EMERSON'S ORIENTALISM

By the Same Author

Literary (Poetry)

Desert Blooms (Writers' Workshop, Kolkata, 1987)

Echoes Silent (Writers' Workshop, Kolkata, 1988)

The Images of a Growing Dying City (Writers' Workshop, Kolkata, 1989)

Small Reflections (Writers' Workshop, Kolkata, 2000)

Voice of the Valley (Minerva Publishing House, New Delhi, 2003)

Wisdom of the Peepal Tree (Minerva Publishing House, New Delhi, 2003)

Samarpana (Reliance Publishing House, New Delhi, 2006)

Non-literary (Yoga)

Yoga for Peace (Abhinav Publications, New Delhi, 2006)

Yoga and Zen (Sharada Publishing House, New Delhi, 2007)

EMERSON'S ORIENTALISM

K.V. Raghupathi

Prestige

an international publishing house

Published by
Prestige Books
C 3/1, Janakpuri
New Delhi 110 058

Ph. 25507139, 9818755529
Email: prestigebooks@gmail.com
Website: www.asiabookclub.com

ISBN: 81-7551-190-7

Printed at Chaman Offset Press, New Delhi 110 002

Contents

Preface

For me, Emerson has been a perennial source of inspiration since my student days. For me, he is more than a literary figure. Even if he were to be treated and regarded as a man of letters, I would say unhesitantingly, the whole of American literature minus him is nothing. Also, Emerson, I personally feel, cannot be viewed as a philosopher. He was not a philosopher in the strictest academic sense. He had never speculated anything. He did not formulate any theory or doctrine or ism nor even ideas. He was essentially a religious man to the core, a spiritual personality, a mystic poet who had experienced the presence of Higher Laws intuitively. His transcendentalism was merely a reassertion of what the oriental mystics had experienced. That is, the Universal Laws can be comprehended only through intuition based on the principle of Self-Reliance and not through intellect.

Emerson discovered India. He drew enormous spiritual inspiration from the Oriental thought, especially Indian thought and philosophy. For Emerson, India was a mysterious symbol, a symbol that had many complex shades of meaning. He recognized the profound wisdom and truth given by the great sages and *rishis* (the seers) of Ancient India. He realized and confessed that the Universal Soul which is impersonal in character and beauty can be realized by man through intuition devoid of all sense experiences. He affirmed that one must reach out to the core of religions, the impersonal within and that impersonal is the creative power of evolution which had been at work ever since the beginning of creation. By contacting this impersonal power within, one receives the needed strength, courage, hope and faith to become an achiever. His subject is man, his ideal is man's happiness on earth, and man's transformation into a divine personality is his goal.

There is literally an explosion of neurosis in the Western world and in order to alleviate their personal problems, people resort to psychotherapists. The solution does not lie in material benefits but realizing one's mental potentialities in rediscovering his lost harmony with cosmos and in transcending loneliness by looking into ourselves. It is here Emerson has immense relevance and profound significance in the context of deterioration of moral values and spiritual values in the society. Denying Emerson is denying mankind. Accepting Emerson is accepting one's own existential predicament and overcoming it by recognizing and realizing one's true nature, that is pure, unsullied and divine.

The present study *Emerson's Orientalism* demonstrates the central influence of Vedantic thought on the writings of Emerson. It is a comprehensive study of the precise impact of Vedantic concepts like *Paramatman*, *Maya*, *Karma*, *Nityatva* and *Sahaja Jnana* on Emerson. The philosophic system existing in Emerson is very close to the Vedantic philosophical system. The purpose of the study is to show the influence and impact of Vedantic philosophy on Emerson and draw striking parallels between Emerson's thought and Vedantic thought. In dealing with this, the main emphasis is laid on Vedantic influence and not on Persian, Sufi, Chinese and Buddhist influences.

The study is divided into six chapters. The first chapter, "From Calvinism to Transcendentalism," serves as an introduction to the major developments in American philosophy before the Civil War, from the early Puritanism to New England Transcendentalism. This early period, extending roughly from 1700 to 1860, includes three important representatives, Jonathan Edwards as representative of Puritanism, Thomas Jefferson as representative of American Enlightenment and Ralph Waldo Emerson as representative of New England Transcendentalism. Significantly, these philosophers found their new ideas of freedom and progress and the urgency of commitments to beliefs on the part of individual person for creating and achieving peace and happiness.

In the second chapter entitled "Search for a Worldview," an attempt is made to trace various influences that shaped and moulded Emerson's thought and philosophy. The influences are many and varied, and they include the earliest influences comprising family and books, and writers, major influences like German idealists, English Romanticists, Plato and Neo-Platonists, Quakers, and Oriental thought and philosophy.

The third chapter with the title "Emerson and Vedanta" is devoted to the study of Emerson's orientalism, chiefly the influence of Ancient Indian thought comprising the Vedanta philosophy. It is divided into five sub-sections, and in each a particular concept is taken up to draw parallels between Emerson's thought and Vedantic thought. An attempt is also made to study in brief the Vedantic philosophy and thought, the chief foundation of Indian thought and tradition.

In the fourth chapter, "Idealism and Spirituality," Emerson's idealism and spiritualism is examined in detail in the context of Vedantic idealism and spiritualism. His idealism implies that the phenomenal world is not the ultimate reality; spiritualism is its constant realization from moment to moment.

In the fifth chapter, "Mysticism," particular attention is paid on the concepts of pantheism and mysticism which are inherent in Emerson's philosophy. It is justified and proved from his journals and essays and poems that Emerson had undergone, in the true sense of a mystic, spiritual experiences. He often stated that his ego was dissolved and merged with the Universal Being. He valued his mystical experiences above all others as they provided an insight into life.

In the concluding chapter, "Revaluation," an attempt is made to revalue the oriental influence on Emerson, his ideas and thoughts and his contribution to American philosophy and literature.

Finally, I express my deep sense of gratitude to all those who helped and assisted me directly or indirectly in executing this work.

K.V. RAGHUPATHI

Chapter I

From Calvinism to Transcendentalism

The purpose of this chapter is to study the major developments in American philosophy before the Civil War, the climate of ideas in which Emerson worked. This early period, extending roughly from 1700 to 1860, was dominated by three important thinkers, Jonathan Edwards as the representative of Puritanism, Thomas Jefferson as the champion of American Enlightenment and Ralph Waldo Emerson as the leader of New England Transcendentalism. All the three ideas had already been worked out in Europe. For these philosophers, the practical affairs of life, of surviving and progressing, took precedence over thought and new speculation. They reflected the urgency of commitments to beliefs on the part of individual for creating and achieving freedom worth to be imitated and emulated by all. However much they may have differed in what they believed, all endorsed an unwavering commitment to what each took to be the greatest good.

Calvinism and Determination

The Calvinists were extremely rigid and pious. The eighteenth century America was completely dominated by Calvinists who were preaching the rigid form of religion, and people were under their influence, irresistant. The philosophy of Calvinists was simple but harsh and coercive. It taught that men, even at birth, were depraved and despicable objects, and as such were to be watched, herded, suspected and regulated until death. It was harsh, theocratic, autocratic and dogmatic. The spirit of Calvinism was widespread and it had taken possession of the Presbyterian Methodists and Baptist churches. The Calvinists were seek-

other religious views. This contradiction coupled with the strong differences of opinion about church, government gradually led to the decline of strict, theocratic Puritanism or Calvinism by the first half of the eighteenth century.

Precisely, at this time of strongest internal conflict and decline, Jonathan Edwards (1703-1758) gave his stoutest philosophical defence to American Calvinism. Edwards had his lifelong career as a minister of the gospel in the strictest Calvinist sense. Throughout his active career as a clergyman and preacher of hell-fire sermons, Edwards justified the majesty of the divine being, the total depravity and predestination of man, and the glorious work of the redemption of man through divine grace. This three-pronged idea of Puritanism permeated Edward's system of thought. Edwards' was the uncompromising Calvinist Puritanism. Calvinist Christianity required an unflinching adherence to definite, firmly decided principles, from the absolute majority and rule of the divine being to the utter depravity and determination of the will of man.

According to Edwards' theism, God, as the creator, is the absolute ruler of the world. So, this forms as separation between God and His creation. The divine being is characterized by omnipotence, omniscience, and perfect benevolence while the world is temporal, limited and totally dependent on God. With the fall of Adam, men were left in such a state of sin and depravity that they were powerless to perform any truly good actions or salvage their damaged souls. Only with the assistance of God can man be saved. Man's will is so depraved that only a determination of it by a divine source can redeem it. So, according to this theism, divine grace is absolutely essential for man to salvage himself. It convicts man as an eternal sinner. God is under no obligation to save every sinner, but miraculously elects a few for saintliness as a free gift of his divine grace. To Edwards, this meant that all men are bound to suffer an eternal damnation. The hopelessness of man can be realized through prayer for divine help and deliverance.

Edwards formulated his theism in the most rigid terms and made it an all-inclusive doctrine. He was convinced that he was right and realistic and communicated his definiteness to others. He defended his beliefs against the strong attacks of deists, Armenians.[1] He kept up his beliefs through his major philosophical and theological writings against the encroachments of rationalism. He resolved to set out his pure Calvinist position, the inevitable conclusions of his doctrine, demolishing all other alternatives with ruthless logic. For Edwards, a determination from a higher source is needed to explain man's creation. He argued that absolute nothing is a logical impossibility. Therefore, there must be an absolute something, an all-comprehending being.

His leading principle was that all things are ultimately determined by an eternal, infinite, and perfect source or cause. He even used it to explain the final cause of evil and man's depraved condition. He believed that man could not be depraved unless the infinite power of God permitted it. The divine being is not the direct cause of man's evil ways, but rather the indirect cause of them. Men are deprived of pure love and necessary will power to achieve it. The divine will is determined by the most perfect and holy motives. God necessarily chooses what is perfectly good and virtuous. Man, on the other hand, by necessity chooses or wills what is imperfectly good or not really good at all.

Edwards succeeded in articulating a carefully consistent philosophical system. In his epistemology, he began with an empirical framework and derived a metaphysical idealism and coherent theory of truth. He drew the conclusion that all ideas of so-called "extremely existing material things" must depend upon the experience of mind. So, according to Edwards, the material world is known to us only through our ideas,. and can only be known to exist mentally. Truth itself can reside nowhere but in the mind. He says truth is the perception of the "relation between ideas that are inconsistent with those ideas themselves; not their disagreement with things without."[2]

Edwards formulated these ideas very early in life and throughout his career he preached and propagated them resolutely, decisively and piously. As a young student at Yale, he discovered the ideas of the English philosopher John Locke and the great scientist Isaac Newton. Locke provided him with the inspiration that all knowledge must come from experience, and Newton provided a basis for Edwards to argue the universal causation of all things. Nevertheless, Edwards was defending, during his lifetime, a decaying world outlook. Puritanism, by the first half of the eighteenth century, was dying out. By 1750 the forces of the American Enlightenment were sufficiently strong to encourage abandonment of the Puritan worldview.

Philosophically, Edwards was neither followed nor refuted. He was neglected. Though he stands as the most articulate spokesman of early American Puritanism, his philosophical views on freedom of will, true virtue, the mind, and the religious affections made little impact on philosophical thought in America. Historically, he was associated with all the narrowness and moral fanaticism of the movement he defended, and his philosophic tradition. George Santayana[3] associated Edwards with "the religion of the agonized conscience." Though he was the first systematic theologian-philosopher that America has produced, his Calvinism, with its deep sense of sin and hope of salvation, encouraged hard work and then paved the way for enlightenment, growth, and prosperity. Calvinism thus lost its basis in American life.[4]

Enlightenment and Freedom

By 1750 the seeds of the Enlightenment and the struggle for independence began to sprout. The founding fathers, Benjamin Franklin and Thomas Jefferson, were interested in enlightenment, liberty, the pursuit of human happiness and the practical wisdom rather than speculative theology. This practical wisdom they imbibed from the "free thinkers" of the European Enlightenment. Francis Bacon (1561-1626), Isaac Newton (1642-1727) and John Locke (1632-1764) were primary sources of knowledge and inspiration for the leaders of the American Enlightenment.

During the middle of the eighteenth century, America needed not God-centred philosophy but a practical, social and political philosophy which could provide progress for the betterment of mankind. Thomas Jefferson (1743-1826) supplied this need better than any other man. Jefferson was and is the philosopher par excellence of American democracy. He was both a skilful architect and a tireless builder of the new American Republic. He might best be compared to the Roman Emperor and philosopher Marcus Amelicus as one of the few individuals in history who have achieved intellectual as well as political eminence. Jefferson conceived the life of the new, struggling Republic in broader humanistic terms than any one else of his age. He expressed in his thoughts and carried through in his activities all the principal concerns of the American Enlightenment.

He brought the intellectual activities of French cultural life and many ideas of the leading philosophers and scientists of Europe to his country by way of Enlightenment. The American Enlightenment represents an interesting reaction to Puritanism. The growth of urban population and life and the fundamental freedom of man had put an end to the provincial and religiously authoritarian Puritanism. The chief concern of the Enlightenment was for religious freedom. Jefferson was an outspoken crusader for religious freedom. He asserted, "I can never join Calvin in addressing *his God* . . . his religion was daemonism. If ever man worshipped a false God, he did."[5] His strong opposition to Calvinist theism was based on his concerns for human freedom, happiness and the growth of practical knowledge. Calvinism considered man depraved, was intolerant of other religious views, and placed miracle and revelation ahead of reason and experiment. Jefferson, as an advocate of deism, considered man good and perfectible, stood for religious tolerance and favoured the growth of natural knowledge.

Deism asserts, in opposition to Calvinist theism, that religion is based on human reason and observation rather than on revelation or miracle. This natural religion, as it was called, held that the natural powers of man are sufficient to reveal the divine being in all the laws and parts of nature. For deism the existence of a divine being is required as a creator of the universe, and the universe is conceived as orderly and rational, changing in accordance with natural laws. Once created with orderly laws, nature accounts for all occurrences. Jefferson, in defending deistic views, gave expression to this fundamental concern for the well-being and progress of man. Deism was the form of religion that was open to the growth of new knowledge; it was chiefly humanistic. Calvinism was for the elect. Deism was open to all men.

The American Enlightenment was also devoted to political freedom. Just as religious freedom implied a sense of man's importance and essential goodness, so political freedom involved an awareness of man's right to self-government. As a man of Enlightenment, Jefferson was a leader in the cause of political liberty and self-determination. His confidence in the people to decide their own manner of government was based on his optimistic view of the possibilities latent within human nature. He viewed political freedom as both a natural right and a continuing experiment. According to John Dewey, Jefferson "was the first modern to state in human terms the principles of democracy."[6] This means that he was indeed a practical philosopher. Since he viewed democracy in broadly human and common sense terms, the "issues Jefferson raised are still of fundamental importance for our life and times."[7] A man's freedom cannot be infringed upon without denying the essential worth, perfectibility, or goodness of mankind. According to Jefferson, enlightenment and freedom had to be taken together. Unless men were educated and enlightened, he felt, their freedom would either bring on mob rule or be easily dissipated. And unless men were free to inquire, form their opinions, and test their hypotheses, they could never be enlightened.

Rationalism is fundamental in Jefferson's thought process. In his view, men in society could devise orderly ways of pursuing their mutual well-being through reason and experiment. Political and religious freedom could come under the guidance of reason which could benefit mankind. Deism was for him a religion of reason; democracy was simply the politics of reason. Further, the Enlightenment view held that knowledge is common knowledge. Knowledge cannot be esoteric and at the same time serve any humanitarian purpose. The Enlightenment philosopher, according to Jefferson, must be a universal man. He cannot separate political ideas from ideas of science; he cannot compartmentalize his learning or experience, nor become an expert in just one sub-division, all knowledge worthy of the name must contribute to man's progress. Basic in Enlightenment thought was the view that the growth of science and education implied human progress. This theme of Enlightenment and freedom are central to Jefferson's view of man and his whole conception of philosophy. His vigorous maintaining of them had made him the most perfect embodiment of Enlightenment philosophy that America produced.

Thomas Jefferson's lifetime spans the entire period from Jonathan Edwards to Ralph Waldo Emerson, from the end of Puritanism to the beginning of Transcendentalism in New England. Consequently, he had influenced the American mind enormously and impressively in dramatic grandeur. For generations of Americans, he has become a symbol of human freedom, the individual rights of man, and all that is progressive and good in a democratic way of life. Jefferson's liberalism was combined with an equally strong realism. His high regard for individual freedom could not be obtained without struggle or without maintaining a sense of social justice and responsibility. He embodied the maxims of independent and comprehensive thought, encouraged naturalistic, pragmatic and common sense tendencies found in later philosophers.

Although Jefferson advocated and extolled individual freedom, reason, science and democracy, as a philosophy of life Enlightenment was left unfinished. Based on common sense and practical affairs, American Enlightenment defined the dignity and good of the individual in external and social terms rather than in internal or autonomous ones. By the end of Jefferson's life, the need had arisen for a more imaginative and individualistic philosophy of life. This was provided by the New England Transcendentalists who marked the third major phase of early American philosophy.

Transcendentalism and Self-Reliance

The Enlightenment has supplied reason and freedom which fostered social and political advance in America, but what was still needed was an affirmation of the moral and spiritual value of the individual. The Enlightenment has freed men from oppression, superstition and ignorance. But the question remained whether this social and political advance would make the individual true to himself. This assertion of man's unfettered allegiance to himself was given by Transcendentalism.

Transcendentalism in New England came into existence as a form of revolt against Calvinism that took shape in the rise of Unitarianism.[8] Grounded in deistic rationalism, it was able to attack Calvinism with cold logic. Accepting the authority of human reason of John Locke, the Unitarians rejected the miraculous and denied not only the Trinity but also the divinity of Jesus and the authority of the Bible as the unquestionable word of God. The Unitarians held that Jesus was a man, and therefore not divine, and that Christianity was not a series of creeds or definitions, but a way of life. According to them, man is a progressive spiritual creature who continues to develop even after death. On the point of salvation, Unitarians were equally consistent. According to them, sin is a matter of morality, involving human relationships, and is not an offence against God. Man is responsible for his acts, and few ever achieve complete goodness in this life.

The Bible is not finite, but is only one of the many possible avenues to truth, and is real for ethics rather than for theology. The Church is purely a human institution, and no single Church has any monopoly on the means of salvation. Since God has made man in his own image, man partakes also of the divine goodness. The greatest moral force here on earth is to be found in the example of the lives of noblemen. The sacraments of Baptism and the Lord's Supper are regarded as simply memorials.

Nominally, the Unitarian dissent was over the doctrine of the Trinity. But Hutchinson[9] has observed that it was realistically over the nature of man and his ability to contribute to his own salvation. Central to the Unitarians' creed was its doctrine of human nature rather than its doctrine of God.[10] Man, they held, possessed an infinite capacity for good, of which Jesus, a man rather than a God, was a prime exemplar.

So appealing was this doctrine that by 1785 King's Chapel, the Anglican Church in Boston, became openly Unitarian, and by 1815 fourteen of the sixteen pre-revolutionary Boston congregational churches had followed suit. Stephen Whicher called it the marriage of New England Puritanism and the Enlightenment.[11] Curiously enough, Unitarianism had captured Harvard College, most of the important Boston pulpits and churches of the larger American towns. In 1819 William Ellery Channing became the spokesman and new leader of the Unitarians. Channing fought vigorously to rid Unitarianism of what he called its "union with a heart-withering philosophy," and to open the floodgates of poetry and religious fervour. He revitalized Unitarianism by preaching and the example of irreproachable personal character, and also did the ground work for the moral and spiritual basis of Transcendentalism, the movement for which Emerson was to be the chief spokesman.

The emancipation of Unitarianism from theological despotism was complete. It became Christianity without Christ. It was almost a religion without God. Nevertheless, Unitarianism did not really make the man true to himself. Its mild yoke was oppressive to sensitive spirits who could soar higher, faster if unfettered altogether. The cold rationalism of Unitarianism was another restraining factor. This had prompted the Transcendental protest made in the name of broader self-determination in the spiritual life of the individual.

By the early 1830s, the transcendentalists headed by Emerson had brought a poetic, highly romantic focus to the problem of the meaning and purpose of man's life.

Transcendentalism marks an important reaction against the period of Enlightenment, and against materialism and orthodoxy as well. It may be viewed as part of the larger romantic movement. As Merle Curti observed, "It was a revolt against the rationalism of the 18th century. It emphasized those aspects of man's nature that were said to transcend or be independent of experience."[12] The chief characteristic features of romantic movement were the delight in, and wonder at, the beauty and beneficence of nature, the recognition of the individual human being as superior to society, the concomitant objection to social restraints upon the individual, and, above all, the ascendancy of emotion and intuitive perception over reason. Faith becomes the primary source of knowledge, and the creativity of man is stressed.

Transcendentalism in America was derived chiefly from three sources, namely, the German Idealists, the English Romanticists and the Oriental Literature and philosophy. The German Romanticists like Goethe, Herder and Kant held that experience is much broader than the reason of the Enlightenment; consequently they revolted against the empiricism of Locke and the scepticism of Hume. Immanuel Kant's *Critique of Pure Reason* could be seen as the philosophical high watermark of their revolt against the rationalists. It was Kant who first employed the word "transcendental" which was later borrowed by New England Transcendentalists with an important change in the meaning. Hutchinson notes that the transcendental philosophy that was given by Kant in the *Critique* was a systematic exposition of the nature of a priori knowledge.[13] Central to this thesis is the idea that the mind is superior to matter; that the mind is endowed with elemental concepts and forms of intuition that cannot be derived through inductive logic. Emerson asserts that Kant succeeded in "showing that there was a very important class of ideas or imperative which experience was acquired; that these were intuitions of the mind itself; and he denominated them as Transcendental forms. The extraordinary profoundness and precision of that man's thinking have given vogue to this nomenclature, in Europe and America, to that extent that whatever belongs to the class of intuitive thought is popularly called as the present day Transcendental."[14]

Frothingham in his book *Transcendentalism in New England* admirably sums up the successive contributions of Jacobi, Fichte and Schelling and suggests that the "idealists of New England were largest debtors to Jacobi and Fichte."[15] Accepting Frothingham's observation, Curti views American Transcendentalism as "spiritual and practical rather than metaphysical."[16].

For American Transcendental movement, however, at least in the earlier stage, the influence came from the English Romantic movement by way of Coleridge, Carlyle and Wordsworth. Coleridge, who had lived and studied in Germany, was the most influential. He distinguished between Understanding and Reason, a distinction that Emerson equated Understanding with science or knowledge, reason with wisdom, a revelation that comes only through deep feeling or intuition. Carlyle, yet another great English philosopher, who came under the influence of German philosophy and literature, also provided tremendous stimulus to American Transcendentalism with his *Sartor Resartus* which Emerson in his enthusiasm had published in the United States after Carlyle had vainly sought a British publisher. As Tony Tanner has observed, "three of Emerson's key ideas received tremendous impetus from Carlyle's work."[17] They are the need for an attitude of wonder in viewing nature; a conviction that every object, even the smallest, is a symbol of God; and a rejection of history in favour of "the everlasting NOW." Wordsworth also provided impetus to the Transcendentalists with his romantic belief that childhood is "a visionary state to which man should attempt to return."[18] The child in his uneducated state is innocent, divine and pure, and endowed with pristine feeling of the organic wholeness of the Universe, wonder and delight that is not weakened by the intellectual activity of logical analysis that comes with education and learning. Hence, the child is the father of man, a true philosopher, and man must return to this lost state in order to be one with the universe and nature and peaceful and happy. This repeated emphasis made by Wordsworth upon the child of nature as the only true philosopher is echoed again and again in the literature of the American Transcendentalists, with Emerson and Whitman its most brilliant expositors.

The final major influence of Transcendentalism in America is the oriental thought and philosophy. Arthur Christy's book *The Orient in American Transcendentalism* provides convincing evidence of American interest in the Orient, which began with the China trade so profitably engaged in by numerous new England merchants. This trade which turned from merely economic to the spiritual and moral provided the change that coincided with the growth of the Transcendental Movement. Emerson, Thoreau and Whitman were the chief expositors who had drawn enormous inspiration from reading the Oriental classics, religious and philosophical works. Indeed Carpenter suggests that Emerson, Thoreau and Whitman started a movement toward Orientalism that expanded rapidly in American literature.[19] But Carpenter also makes the important point that Emerson remained Occidental while reinterpreting the Oriental books.[20] Wishburn shows that the Transcendentalists were "the first group in the United States to seize upon and popularize the translations of Oriental works. . . . The Vedas, the Upanishads, the *Mahabharata*, the Code of Manu, Buddha, Confucius, Mencius, the Koran, the Persian poets, all passed before their eyes and received their enraptured praise."[21]

Transcendentalism was fostered by such writers and thinkers as R.W. Emerson, H.D Thoreau, Bronson Alcott, George Ripley, Orestes Brownson, W.H. Changing, Samuel Johnson, Moncure Daniel Conway and a few others. These writers and thinkers, most of them clergymen, propagated their ideas and thoughts through the Transcendental Club, the name given by the public, which was started in 1836. It provided as a forum in which ideas were explored, reactions noted, and encouragement provided. Revelation, inspiration, providence, law and truth were among the topics openly treated and discussed. If the members exhibited any tendency in common in their discussion, it was a pantheistic view of life.[22] These transcendentalists were primarily preachers who translated their philosophy into practice. This they did not only through sermons, but also through schools, conversations, lecturing, the writing of essays, and participation in reform movements. They were one in feeling that their country was advancing rapidly in exactly the wrong direction. It was not that they were opposed to the idea of progress. But, progress, according to them, was not truly progress unless it was directed aright. As Ekrich clearly puts it: "In the minds of Emerson and the transcendentalists, the progress of society depended primarily upon the improvement of its individual members."[23] Mind, according to them, must gain the ascendancy over matter.

The transcendentalists believed in the exaltation of man, the idea that all power and wisdom come from nature, with which man must form a first-hand relationship, the relegation of books to a secondary place in the scale of values, and the instinct that is good and must be obeyed rather than curbed by convention and authority. Thus, they dealt with the fundamental issues of human life, which were characterized by a soaring idealism. As Curti observed, their seeking and glorification of the individual corresponded to the democratic doctrine that all men possess a sacred right to govern themselves to reach for the stars.[24] Odell Shepard's observation that "transcendentalism was in essence a philosophy and a religion of reform"[25] is indubitably true. Indeed, Ekrich sees it as the popular reform philosophy of the 1840s.[26]

Emerson, the chief spokesmen of Transcendental philosophy in America, breathed a new and essentially romantic meaning in his philosophy. Following Coleridge and other romanticists, Emerson used "intuition" to signify the poetic faculty of seeing things creatively, seeing things with a freshness and richness such as only the widest exercise of imagination could contemplate. Therefore, Emerson can say: "The sensual man conforms thoughts to things; the poet conforms to his thoughts."[27] The poet, because of his creativeness, is by nature a transcendentalist or idealist, since he is truly self-reliant. Rather than conform his ideas to things, he makes things conform to his ideas. The poet makes his vistas or world from his imagination, or from the intuition of the mind itself. Intuition suggests a direct seeing by the mind, reason suggests a comprehension or knowing by the mind, and imagination suggests a fabrication or creating of things known.

Emerson's transcendentalism is therefore simply "romantic idealism." As he says: "What is popularly called transcendentalism among us, is Idealism; Idealism as it appears in 1842."[28] For Emerson, romantic idealism implies both a fresh and a comprehensive outlook on all things. Religiously, it implies pantheism; morally, it implies self-reliance or individualism; and, as an outlook on nature and society as well, it signifies spiritualism and mysticism.

Emerson asserted that it is through the intuitive powers of men's souls that the divine and moral reality finds a unity. The more self-reliant or self-existent a soul, the more divine it is. The more self-reliant or integrity-bound it is, the more it aspires to the highest moral goals. Individuality, for Emerson, means fullness of self, a realization of the infinite universal self. The more truly individual man is, the more he is a whole man, a harmony of complementary parts. Thus, the unity in Emerson's transcendentalism indicates mysticism. Mysticism not only involves the assertion that the soul of man and the divine reality are capable of union or oneness, it also involves the assertions that both are infinite or essentially without limitations, and that the achievement of oneness is possible only through intuition or indirect knowledge of the truth. It is in this sense that Emerson stands as the best exponent of Transcendentalism—not merely because he formulated its ideology more coherently than any other romantic, but by the manner in which he succeeded in trying his thoughts together to exhibit, simply and poetically, the inspiring character of the transcendental position. In short, he brought transcendentalism "out into the world" in such a way as to reach a wider audience than any other transcendentalist.

In the words of Octavis B. Frothingham, "the transcendental movement was an important factor in American life."[29] It set the tone of intellectual, moral and spiritual—for an entire generation of Americans, and its impact can be felt even to the present day. Frothingham calls it "a distinct philosophical system,"[30] that was "essentially poetical."[31] Frederic I. Carpenter, on the other hand, maintains that American Transcendentalism was "primarily a re-assertion of the mystical basis of all religion" and was therefore "primarily religious rather than philosophical."[32] H.C. Goddard sees it as a literary movement, a philosophy and a religion all in one.[33] Walter L. Leighton calls it "the doctrine that man has a knowledge of philosophic principles by an immediate beholding without the process of reason or aid of experience."[34] Kenneth Walter Cameron describes it most succinctly as "a warm and intuitional religious, aesthetic, philosophical and ethical movement—the American tributary of European Romanticism—a theoretical and practical way of life and a literary expression within the tradition of "Idealism"—a new humanism based upon ancient classical or Neo-Platonic supernaturalism and coloured by Oriental mysticism."[35] Emerson in his Boston Lecture of 1842, "The Transcendentalist" simply called it, "Idealism as it appears in 1842."[36] What emerges from all these observations is that Transcendentalism which flourished during 1830s and 1860s was highly subjective and individualistic in nature that made it distinct and inestimable in the history of American literature and philosophy.

NOTES

1. The Armenians began as a Dutch religious sect who took their name from Jacobas Arminus (1560-1609). Their influence spread to England, and by 1734 they were gaining many converts in America. Edwards, in fact, viewed them as a serious threat to Calvinism, since the Armenians believed in the freedom or self-

determining power of man's will. This implied that man could freely choose to sin or not to sin which in turn implied a denial of man's predestination or absolute dependence on God.

2. Jonathan Edwards, "The Mind," in Vergilius Ferm, ed., *Puritan Sage: Collected Writings of Jonathan Edwards*, p. 17.
3. Guy W. Stroh, *American Philosophy from Edwards to Dewey* (Princeton, 1960), p. 209.
4. George Santayana, *Winds of Doctrine and Platonism and the Spiritual Life*, p. 191.
5. "Thomas Jefferson" in Adrienne Koch and William Peden, ed. *The Life and Selected Writings of Thomas Jefferson*, pp. 705-6. From "Letter to John Adams," Monticello, April 11, 1823.
6. John Dewey, *Freedom and Culture* (New York, 1939), p. 155.
7. Sidney Hook, *The Paradoxes of Freedom* (Berkley: University of California Press, 1964), p. 1.
8. Goddard, *Studies in New England Transcendentalism* (New York, 1908), p. 185.
9. Hutchinson, *The Transcendental Ministers*, p. 3.
10. *Ibid.*, p. 5.
11. Stephen E. Whicher, *Freedom and Fate: An Inner Life of Ralph Waldo Emerson* (Philadelphia, 1953), p. 7.
12. Merli Curti, *The Growth of American Thought* (New York, 1951), p. 304.
13. Hutchinson, *The Transcendental Ministers*, p. 24.
14. "The Transcendentalist," *The Complete Essays and Other Writings of Ralph Waldo Emerson*, ed. Brooks Atkinson, p. 93.
15. O.B. Frothingham, *Transcendentalism in New England* (New York, 1976), p. 46.
16. *The Growth of American Thought*, p. 304.
17. Tony Tanner, *The Reign of Wonder: Naivety and Reality in American Literature* (New York, 1967), p. 9.
18. *Ibid.*, p. 5.
19. Frederic I. Carpenter, *Emerson and Asia* (Cambridge, 1930), pp. 250-51.
20. *Ibid.*, p. 26.
21. Wilcomb E. Washburn, "The Oriental Roots of American Transcendentalism," *The Southern Journal*, IV, No. IV (1949), p. 141.
22. Lidsay Swift, *Brook Farm: Its Members, Scholars and Visitors* (New York and London, 1900), p. 9.

23. Arthur A. Ekrich, *The Idea of Progress in America, 1815-1860* (New York, 1944), p. 158.
24. *Growth of American Thought*, p. 304.
25. Odell Shepard, *Pedlar's Progress: The Life of Bronson Alcott* (Boston, 1937), p. 268.
26. Arthur A. Ekrich, *The Idea of Progress in American, 1815-1860*, p. 155.
27. "Nature" from *The Complete Essays and Other Writings of Ralph Waldo Emerson*, p. 29.
28. *Ibid.*, p. 87, from "The Transcendentalist."
29. *Transcendentalism in New England* (New York, 1959), p. XXV.
30. *Ibid.*, p. 136.
31. *Ibid.*, p. 138.
32. F.I. Carpenter, *Emerson Handbook* (New York, 1953), pp. 128-29.
33. Harold Clarks Goddard, *Studies in New England Transcendentalism* (New York: 1908)
34. Walter L. Leighton, *French Philosophers and New England* (Charlottesville, Va., 1908), p. 5.
35. Kenneth Walter Cameroon, *Young Emerson's Transcendental Vision: An Exposition of His Worldview with an Analysis of the Structure, Backgrounds, and Meaning of Nature* (1836; Hartford, 1971), p. 7.
36. Ralph Waldo Emerson, *The Journals and Miscellaneous Notebooks* (Cambridge, Mass., 1964, VIII), p. 313.

Chapter II

Search for a Worldview

Transcendentalism represents the literary phase of early American philosophy, during which philosophy was in the hands of the poet-philosopher, Ralph Waldo Emerson. This form of philosophy in America is romantic, involving an imaginative attempt to set man free from all restrictions and view him as purely self-reliant and creative. Emerson believed in the existence of Universal Soul, the true animating principle of Cosmos, the unifying principle of man, nature and god. According to him this Universal Soul is impersonal in character and beauty, and the centre of all creation. Man being at the peak of existence can realize this not through experience based on senses but through intuition, devoid of all experience. The heightened self-awareness—the mind's recognition of itself in all that it notes—is what Emerson terms intuition. Only intuition can comprehend the reality, and that reality is infinitely rich and beautiful. Emerson holds forth intuition as embodiment of the quality of genius in all men. Therefore, the more self-reliant man is, the more intuitive; the more self-aware of the One Principle animating the whole Cosmos, the more Godly; the more unified and integrated, the more optimistic and the more blissful he is. This self-aware man romantically aspires to be without restrictions—infinite and free. This constitutes the core and essence of Emerson's thought and philosophy.

This profound realization did not come to Emerson spontaneously or in a mood of sudden inspiration, but gradually over a span of fifty years, from the youthful observations of his adolescence to the scepticism of his middle years and, finally, to the mature and balanced view of life of his later years, based on the major principle of his philosophy, the concept of self-reliance. In this chapter, an attempt is made to study various influences that shaped and moulded Emerson's thought and philosophy. The influences are many and varied.

The Earliest Influences: Family

The earliest influences came from his family. On the paternal side, Emerson's father was a Puritan clergyman. He died while Waldo was still a small boy. He was a man of pleasing and affable personality and of marked liberality of belief and spirit. Emerson's mother was a woman "of great patience and fortitude, of the serenest trust in God, of a discerning spirit, and a most courteous bearing. . . . Both her mind and her character were of a superior order, and they set their stamp upon manners of peculiar softness and natural grace and quiet dignity."[1] At the death of her husband, she struggled bravely to secure the education of her sons. To Emerson, his mother was "a serene, an ennobling presence in the house."[2] With the loss of his father, Emerson had very little time to spend on sports and recreations of boyhood. His youth was one of hard work. His early intellectual training was provided by his aunt, Marry Moody Emerson,[3] a woman of noble thought, of stern character, and of exceptional training. Emerson under her tutorship had learnt to be self-disciplined, and industrious. Her early reading[4] of Milton, Young Akensside, Samuel Clarke, Jonathan Edwards, the Bible, Plato, Plotinus, Marcus Antonius, Stewart, Coleridge, Cousin, Herder, Locke, Madame de Stael, Channing, Mackintosh and Byron showed remarkable quality of knowledge and broad outlook. Emerson bore testimony to her influence on him when he wrote later in life: "I have no hour of poetry or philosophy, since I knew these things, into which she does not enter as a genius."[5] To him and his brother, their aunt was "a spur, or better, a ferment in their young lives."[6]

By a sense, we cannot ignore Emerson's Puritanical attitude in his youthful years. Holmes mentions that by heritage Emerson belonged to the "Brahmin" caste of New England with its deep sense of Puritan righteousness and its agonized conscience. He had descended from seven generations of Puritan ministers. Emerson's earliest interpretations of life, God, universe and nature are a testimony to his predisposition to Puritanism. As a youth, Emerson sought answers from the traditional Christian religion. His observations, his views on God, man, nature, the universe, immortality, society and slavery were based on the Christian religion, and not on insight or intuition as he developed and professed in his later years. Like a Puritan he drew enormous inspiration from the traditional explanations of Christianity. He believed that man must rely on religion in order to understand the universe, God and existence of evil.

Without questioning, Emerson blindly believed that man lives in a God-centred universe, as professed in the Christian religion. Man is helpless and cannot comprehend and hence, he must totally surrender to the will of God. He believed God was personal. He did not give any rational justification to his views. As to the question of immortality, Young Emerson in the early *Journals* referred to life as "Journey to the throne of God,"(I, 210) and "a race of preparation for the eternal world." (I, 285) He believed "in the existence and activity of good beings, and in the promise of rewards accommodated hereafter to the vicious or virtuous dispositions which were cultivated here." (I, 221) Here young Emerson reveals the Christian linear view of life which focuses on life after death and the god of heavens.

On the question of evil, he queried in his early *Journals*: "If God is good, why are any of his creatures unhappy?" (I, 194) Emerson did not attempt to give answer, instead said: "We wisely assure the righteousness of the Creator in placing man in a probationary state. We do not seek with vain ambition to question the abstruse and unreachable ground of this ordination, because it is plain matter of fact that we are incompetent to the discussion." (I, 195) Thus, Emerson expressed the problem of evil which in later years he found difficult to ignore.

Such a Puritanical dependency on traditional Christianity not only affected Emerson's views on God, the soul, after life, but it also greatly influenced his views on man and his role in the society and slavery. The question of man's role in the society has always posed a big problem throughout his life; and as early as in 1822, he began looking not to himself but to the authority of the Bible from which he often quoted, "Love thy neighbour." (*Journals*, I, 227) It was a "prior command" for him and he duly respected it without questioning as it came from "an elder scripture." Because of this command, he added, it is man's duty to live in the society, not in solitude, to help the poor and the miserable. He observed that man must not live in solitude nursing "his own unprofitable existence." (*Journals*, I, 218) He argued that man must bear "his part of the burden of life" and give help to the poor, the sick, the dying.

Thus, it is clear, Emerson in his early years firmly defended the Christian dogma, tradition and authority. In defence of Christianity, he strongly opposed all sceptics and could not even tolerate any individual who rejected Christianity or doubted the existence of the "great power in the Universe." (*Journals*, I, 239) Such "Free thinking" that denies the existence of personalized God which he developed in later years, Emerson argued, like "laughter in the mouth of a maniac." (*Journals*, I, 241)

Books and Writers

Emerson was a bibliophile. His extensive and intensive reading of books helped him shape his thought. In his early years, he took delight in Scott's poetry and Ossian.[7] Of the influences that first and most profoundly helped shape Emerson's thought was recorded from a letter (1841) to Margaret Fuller: "I know but one solution to my nature and relations, which I find in remembering the joy with which in my boyhood I caught the hint of the Berkeleyan philosophy, and which I certainly never lost sight of afterwards."[8] In Raxbury in 1825, he had read Cotton's translations of Montaigne. He recorded: "It seemed to me as if I had written the book myself in some former life, so sincerely it spoke my thought and experience. No book before or since was ever so much to me as that."[9] While in college he was more studious; he was in the classroom found to be more thoughtful and well-read. He had read far more about literature. According to Cabbot, he had read and studied the early English dramatists and poets. He "proved over Montaigne, and knew Shakespeare almost by heart."[10] He reiterates his inconceivable wisdom and "transcendent superiority"[11] over all other writers. He belonged during his sophomore year to a book club that subscribed for the *North American Review* and the leading English periodicals. His notebooks give "evidence of wide reading of a desultory kind, in which history, memoirs, and the English Reviews are prominent."[12] He had also something about his contemporary poets, Byron, Moore, Coleridge and Wordsworth, though the latter two poets had influenced him to undergo a radical change.

Emerson also acquainted himself with German literature and German university methods through his two great teachers, George Thicknor and Edward Everett. He studied Berkeley's philosophy. He knew something of Bacon,[13] Locke, Hume, and Stewart. His reading of two Boudoin prize dissertations on *The Character of Socrates* and *The Present State of Ethical Philosophy* show his interest in metaphysical thought and a knowledge of its history.

Emerson's interest in books continued after college education. Cooke noted, "he early came to love Plato, and, after leaving college, seems to have studied him very closely. At this period Tillotson, Augustine[14] and Jeremy Taylor were among his favourite authors. One of the earliest of the serious books he read was a translation of Pascal's *Pensees*, which he carried to church with him and read almost constantly."[15] While studying divinity Emerson felt to some extent the influence of Dr. Channing who conferred with him occasionally and recommended books for reading. Though the two men never came into intimate contact, Emerson's characterization of Channing as "our Bishop"[16] is a clear recognition of indebtedness. After his trip abroad, he spoke of him as "the king of Preachers,"[17] saying that there were no such men in Great Britain. Of the other transcendentalists, Alcott doubtless had the most significant influence on Emerson.

Emerson's friendship with Alcott increased with the passing of years and flourished to the end. Alcott possessed uniquely a genius for human friendship. Emerson valued Alcott as a source of inspiration. Though Emerson was a bit critical of Alcott's absolute idealism, he repeatedly characterized him as "a tedious archangel," (*Journals*, 21 Nov. 1841) and "a pail without a bottom." Yet Emerson wrote: "I see that I cannot exaggerate its importance among resources of inspiration." (*Journals*, May 1868)

Emerson discovered the younger Thoreau and welcomed him as an "equal,"[18] though the latter towards the end "rejected" the former. Emerson helped him publish his manuscripts, helped him find jobs and continued to praise his works even after Thoreau had withdrawn from intimacy. From 1838 to 1848 the Journals of both men recorded the many walks which they shared. Professor Moore[19] has pointed out that Emerson's *Journals* refer to Thoreau more than twice as often as Thoreau's to Emerson. The two friends, however, drifted apart after Emerson's return from England in 1848. Perhaps the inevitable differences of temperament and opinion such as Thoreau's stubbornness, love of paradox, and bitter humour, or Emerson's idealism, lack of practical skill, and willingness to compromise with society, made them drift apart. But the fact remains that Emerson discovered Thoreau and recognized his greatness before anyone else, that two men enjoyed an intimate and nearly perfect friendship during the most important ten years of their lives, and that Emerson never lost faith in his friend nor allowed bitterness to interfere with his final praise. His essay on Thoreau remains one of the most vivid and human literary pieces, partly because he valued Thoreau so greatly both as a friend and as a writer.

Emerson appreciated Margaret Fuller for the "largeness" of her character. Fuller too had unremitting admiration for Emerson. Her series of visits to his house, her series of letters and books which she sent to him, and her personal services in teaching him German, Goethe and Dante, all contributed to the growing of genius in Emerson. When Alcott and Fuller visited him casually on an evening in October 1839, he noted characteristically in his *Journals*: "Cold as I am, they are almost dear." As their relationship progressed, their virtual influence became great and enthusiastic. Fuller noted: "We had an excellent talk: we agreed that my God was love, his truth."[20] And Emerson noted in his *Journal* in 1843: "I have never known any example of such steady progress from stage to stage of thought and of character." (VI, 364) Their friendship is important for more than personal reasons, because Fuller embodied perfectly one aspect of Emerson's transcendental ideal: "she had large experience." Though Hawthorne violently condemned her, and caricatured her as Zenobia in *The Blithedale Romance*, Emerson praised her, for she "gave all to love."

Emerson formed most of his literary friendships and consciously cultivated them after the age of thirty. Of these his friendships with Carlyle and Thoreau affected significantly the course of literary history. Friendships with Alcott and Margaret Fuller influenced the development of American Transcendentalism; and with Arthur Hugh Clough, John Sterling, and Herman Grimm remained significant in his life.

As regards his general attitude toward books and study, there is no doubt that Emerson loved books and that he read very widely. Indeed, it would hardly be an exaggeration to affirm that a large part of his life was spent in reading. Yet, his own writings would not give the impression of being the work of a learned man or deserve to be mentioned as scholarly. He appears to have used books much more for imbibing the spirit of their writers and extracting felicitous quotations than for studying the details of their thought. He noted, "I read Prochus, and sometimes Plato, as I might read a dictionary, for a mechanical help to the fancy and the imagination. I read for the lusters."[21] He read Plotinus, Goethe, Coleridge, Wordsworth, Carlyle, Swedenborg, the "oriental scriptures" with the same intention and sympathy. This enabled him to comprehend, as it were, in a flash, their points of view. He could think in their ways and so he repeats their thoughts. He writes in his *Journal* for February 8,1825; "My cardinal vice of intellectual dissipation—sinful strolling from book to book, from care to idleness—my cardinal vice still; is a malady that belongs to the chapters of incurables."[22] Elsewhere he expresses a longing for the gift of continuity.[23] A passage from the essay on "Experience" is illuminating: "Once I took such delight in Montaigne that I thought I should not need another book; before that, in Shakespeare; then in Plutarch; then in Plotinus, at one time in Bacon; afterward in Goethe; even in Bettine; but now I turn the pages of genius."[24] His views on the function of books given in the "American Scholar" are vigorous and worthy to be considered: "Meek young men grow up in libraries, believing it their duty to accept the views which Cicero, which Locke, which Bacon have given, forgetful that Cicero, Locke, and Bacon were only young men in libraries, when they wrote books."[25] "Books are the best of things, well used; abused, among the worst. What is the right use? . . . They are for nothing but to inspire."[26] "Man thinking must not be subdued by his instruments. Books are for the scholar's idle times."[27]

Major Influences: German Idealists

Emerson was searching for a worldview which would express in his later years his basic optimistic philosophy based on the principle of self-reliance in comprehending the abstruse truths. For this he derived enormous inspiration and guidance from five major sources. They are German idealist philosophy, English romanticist, Plato and Neo-Platonists, Quakers, and certain Eastern mystical writings which were introduced into the Boston area in the early nineteenth century. The impress of these five major sources was always deep and lasting in the mind of Emerson.

Emerson had read the teachings of Kant and Schilling. Kant's doctrines were the product of reaction against the eighteenth century materialistic philosophy of Locke and Hume who held that one source of knowledge was experience gained by employment of the senses. Kant led the counter-attack for the idealists. He maintained that the senses give us only the appearance of things and true knowledge results from the union of mind and matte, or subject and object. After him came the romantic Schelling who went a step further and declared that subject and object become one in the absolute.

Emerson borrowed the term "transcendentalism" from the German philosopher Kant, but with an important change of meaning. He asserted his position clearly in his *Journals*. Emerson interpreted this term to refer to intuition or direct insight, but for Kant there was no such thing as intuitive knowledge. His notion of the transcendental method is abstract and complex; and this method cannot at all be understood apart from other ideas, equally complex. Kant's system is principally a critical method of analysis and not a method of direct insight. He allowed only two pure intuitions or forms of consciousness, the pure intuition of space and the pure intuition of time. Kant contended that space and time were not themselves ultimate realities, but merely appearances of forms through which experience was ordered or organized by the mind. What Emerson did, therefore, was to take word and leave the idea behind. Further, he popularized transcendentalism in a way that is quite remarkable. He made use of the high-sounding philosophical term to spread a simple doctrine, one that all men could grasp and appreciate. He used the name "transcendentalism" to teach the view that truth is directly revealed to every man if man will only turn within and become truly self-reliant.

English Romanticists

Emerson's transcendentalism was also viewed by historians as a part of the Romantic Movement that started almost all over the West in the nineteenth century. Its immediate source was Coleridge and the English intuitionists. Taking delight in the outward beauty and the beneficent spirit, the healing power of nature, glorification of the individual, strong opposition to such restraints as hinder the flowering of his personality, and the ascendancy of intuition over reason are the main characteristics of Romanticism. It found enthusiastic support from the American Transcendentalists. As Merle Curti points out, Transcendentalism was a revolt against the Rationalism of the eighteenth century and it "emphasized those aspects of man's nature that were said to transcend or be independent of existence."[28]

Like German Idealists, English Romanticists revolted against Locke's empiricism and Hume's scepticism, and maintained that the human mind acquires a certain body of knowledge not through the senses but by transcending them and resorting to intuition. Indeed, German Romantic thought reached the shores of New England not always directly through the writings of Kant and other continental writers but through the interpretation of the English Romanticists, mainly Coleridge, Wordsworth and Carlyle. "At the age of 23, Mr. Emerson had been interested in Coleridge and by him in German thought."[29] In a letter to his aunt dated December 10, 1829, he wrote: "I am reading Coleridge's 'friend' with great interest. . . . He had a tone a little lower than greatness, but what a living soul, what a Universal knowledge."[30] Emerson accepted the distinction made by Coleridge between Understanding (which stands for Science and Knowing) and Reason (which denotes wisdom, a revelation resulting from intuition), and made references to it in his *Nature*.

From the passage devoted to Wordsworth in *English Traits*[31] Emerson considered Wordsworth by far the greatest of the more modern English poets. He admired Wordsworth not as the revolutionary youth who had hailed the French Revolution but for his beautiful poem "Ode on the Intimations of the Immortality." Emerson particularly liked Wordsworth's romantic concept of the child as a "mighty prophet" and "seer blest," and expounded it in several of his writings. "The Ode on Immortality," he wrote, "is the high watermark which the intellect has reached in this age,"[32] and elsewhere, he recorded, "the capital merit of Wordsworth is that he has done more for the sanity of this generation than any other writer."[33] "The fame of Wordsworth," he wrote in the *Dial*, "is a leading fact in modern literature. . . . The excursion awakened in every lover of Nature the right feeling. We saw stars shine, we felt the awe of mountains, we heard the rustle of the wind in the grass, and knew again the ineffable secret of solitude."[34]

Emerson drew great inspiration from Carlyle whom he regarded a philosopher poet. Carlyle came first and remained last. Though Carlyle and Emerson disagreed about most things, they shared and agreed on the fundamental virtue of sincerity or self-reliance. Carlyle inspired Emerson, and welcomed him as an equal at the beginning of his career. Emerson gave Carlyle admiration and faith. It is not a secret that Carlyle the pessimist and sceptic, while valuing Emerson's deeply religious faith, criticized his "moonshiny" optimism. Though they were opposed to each other on many aspects, they complemented each other, admired, respected and loved each other. After Emerson's first visit, Carlyle wrote: "That man came to see me, I don't know what brought him, and we kept him one night, and he left us. I saw him go up the hill . . . and vanish line an angel."[35] Even after eleven years, Carlyle recalled it vividly.[36] Emerson confided in his *Journal* for September 1, 1853: "Carlyle is so amiable that I love him."

His relations with Carlyle are well known through their remarkable friendship and the publication of their correspondence.[37] About the year 1828, Emerson began to be interested in the articles of Carlyle appearing at that time in English and Scotch reviews.[38] The desire to see Carlyle himself was one of the hopes that attracted him to Europe in 1833. In 1836 he published an American edition of *Sartor Resartus* and in 1838 collected some of Carlyle's writings from the reviews and brought them out under the title of *Critical and Miscellaneous Essays*. It was Carlyle who had turned Emerson's interest to German thought and especially to Goethe. Dr. Hedge wrote of Emerson in 1828: "he studied German, mainly for the purpose of acquainting himself with Goethe, to him his attention had been directed by Carlyle."[39] In his letter XII (1836), Emerson wrote to Carlyle: "I read Goethe, and now lately the posthumous volumes, with a great interest."[40] To a letter from Carlyle in 1840, Emerson answered a few weeks later: "You asked me if I read

German, and forget if I have answered. I have contrived to read almost every volume of Goethe, and I have fifty-five, but I have read nothing else: but I have not now looked even into Goethe for a long time."[41]

For Emerson, Carlyle remained a mystic hero poet. Carlyle's writings provided impetus to Emerson's thought and philosophy. Tony Tanner shows how three of Emerson's key ideas received tremendous impetus from Carlyle's work: "The need for an attitude of wonder in viewing Nature; a conviction that every object is a symbol of God, and a rejection of history in favour of "the everlasting NOW."[42] But, later Emerson found Carlyle too worldly, too much devoted to his peculiar kind of economic reform to be achieved through the revival of the medieval system of master and apprenticeship. Nevertheless, the spontaneous, deeply-felt friendship which had joined the two in their youth could not be wholly destroyed by disagreements. When Emerson returned from his third visit to England without staying at Carlyle's house to his native Concord, Emerson noted, "Thomas Carlyle's 80th birthday" among the last entries in his journal. During his final illness, he pointed to Carlyle's picture, and said: "That is my man—my man."[43] Thus, both shared their long friendship though in disagreements.

Plato and Neo-Platonists

Plato's concept of intuition had a major influence on Emerson's thought. The Neo-Platonists and other religious mystics in the same line also influenced Emerson's Transcendentalism. Emerson became acquainted with the writings of Greek philosophers during his student days, and he came to cherish in particular the idealistic thought of Plato. He went to the extent of claiming that "Plato is philosophy, and philosophy, Plato," and remarked that it was a memorable day in a young man's life when he read "The Symposium" for the first time. As Carpenter[44] points out, Plato served two main functions for Emerson: he was "the philosopher" and thus the first of his *Representative*

Men, and he was also "the mystic" who prepared Emerson's mind to receive the religious idealism of the Orient.

Plato resolved the idea of the Supreme Good from which all things are derived and he views the good life as a movement away from the many that change and pass to the One that remains. Emerson's insistence upon the divinity of man and the spiritual character of nature and natural laws derive from his basic mysticism, his Platonism. "Mysticism finds in Plato all its texts."[45] He described Plato as the great mediator between East and West: "The unity of Asia and the detail of Europe . . . Plato came to join, and, by contact, to enhance the energy of each."[46] Emerson's high regard for Plato is based on his finding inexhaustible inspiration and aspiration for man in the Platonic philosophy. Plato, Emerson regarded, is the right teacher for mankind because he maintains that all genuine learning is from within or acquired by self-instruction and that the soul of man has a special affinity for such eternal forms as beauty, justice and truth. Emerson's own mystical pantheism may be seen in Plato. Jefferson regarded Plato's mysticism as unintelligible to the human mind and useless for the practical affairs of life. While Emerson argues, to live with and for only the empirical world is to live without hope, to live without eternal beauty, infinite goodness, or absolute truth. As a transcendentalist, Emerson freely admitted the extravagant nature of Plato's mysticism and never conceived that it could be provided scientifically or experimentally. Plato's romantic conception of man, mysticism, and spiritual laws did not call for proof.

It was Plotinus who taught that the Supreme Good flows ceaselessly outward through Nature and flows back again into itself. The Plotinian concept of emanation, of the "influx of the divine mind into our mind" had contributed to the formation of Emerson's concept of the divinity as the Over Soul. Emerson's belief that the Ultimate Reality can be comprehended only by transcending the limitations of the physical senses and through intuition too its Plotinian and not Platonic idea, and the concept of ecstasy, the mystical union of the human soul with the Divine, is likewise an important teaching of Plotinus. His theory of art as the universal mind working through plastic nature too was ultimately derived from the writings of Plotinus. But Emerson never exalted the mystical experience for its own sake as an end in itself, as did Plotinus and the later Neo-Platonists. His mystical thought is distinctly occidental, Protestant and modern. Thus, he always disagreed with this traditional assumption, and transcended the merely humanistic, or man-centred, point of view.

More specifically, Emerson developed the concept of monism which he derived from Neo-Platonism as the idea of the "correspondence" between moral law and natural law: "The axioms of physics translate the laws of ethics." This idea has been traced both to Neo-Platonism[47] and also to Swedenborg. Finally, Emerson developed from the Neo-Platonists, and not from Plato, his theory that poetry and art may be directly inspired by God, and therefore may express man's highest achievement. Prochus exalted the poet and described his intuitive and symbolic thought as divine. Thus, the Neo-Platonists of Alexandria had made deep and significant influence on Emerson. Emerson found in them the seeds of radical, new ideas.

Quakers

Emerson was also interested in the Quaker doctrine of "the inner light." Specifically, his Transcendentalism had left behind all the forms and traditions of the Unitarian Church, placing its reliance on the conscience, intuition, or "inner light." In his farewell sermon on "The Lord's Supper," Emerson had borrowed many of his arguments against formal religion from the Quakers.[48] In his "Divinity School Address" he rejected "Historical Christianity" itself in favour of "the religious sentiment" in the soul of man. Asked to define his religious position on one occasion, he answered, "I am more of Quaker than anything else. I believe in the 'still, small voice', and that voice is Christ within us."[49]

George Fox, the founder father of Quaker Movement, rejected all ecclesiastical authority and preached men to look for inspiration in the indwelling spirit of God. Thus, he sought to purify the church of the clergy. In a similar way, Emerson moved away from the church towards self-reliant individualism, which he equated with reliance on God. Emerson read Tuke's *Memoirs of the Life of Fox* with considerable interest and enthusiasm and found in him a kindred spirit. Both of them shared the view that religion should be based on an intuitive and personal experience, divorced altogether from hardened traditional forms and authority. The Quakers trusted the individual who could rely more on himself for ethical and spiritual guidance. This implied that man is responsible for his own conduct, that every one is responsible for his present state and that every one is his own friend or enemy.

Oriental Thought and Philosophy

Pantheism, mysticism, and idealism in Emerson's Transcendentalism are identical to Indian philosophy and thought. The Transcendentalists were all disposed towards mysticism at one time or other and had the mystical experience. Carpenter's Rudolph Otto's and Williams James's observation that Emerson was not a mystic in the true sense may be refuted in the face of many available evidences that Emerson had a spiritual experience on more than one occasion. In this first essay "Nature" (1836), he recounts his mystical experience: "Standing on the bare ground,—my head bathed by the blithe air and uplifted into infinite space,—all mean egotism vanishes. I became a transparent eyeball; I am nothing I see all; the currents of the Universal Being circulate through me; I am part or parcel of God."[50] This experience demonstrates that Emerson had the experience of the totality of existence. In another occasion, Emerson speaks like a sage who had the awakening of the Divine. He writes: "A certain wandering light comes to me which I instantly perceive to be the cause of causes." (*Journals*, IV, 248-49) Poems like "Brahma," "Each and All," "Days" and "Hamatreya" and essays like "Over-Soul," "Illusions," "Experience," "Self-Reliance," "Compensation" and "Spiritual Laws" describe mystical experience of high order. Though it may be different to say whether Emerson arrived at a mystic union with God or "an ineffable communion with the Over-Soul,"[51] one may conclude from the evidences in his *Journals* that "his whole mental and spiritual attitude was mystical."[52] Christy is of the opinion that "Emersonian thought was a matter of almost pure mysticism."[53] His idealist monism, his optimism, his rejection of any Christian orthodox and his denial of the reality of evil are the most important areas in which his thought parallels that of the Hindu system.

Emerson was interested in Oriental literature. He had a great admiration and love for Eastern wisdom particularly Hindu philosophy. Christy identifies three components as contributing to the make up of orientalism that influenced Emerson's transcendentalism: "Hindu Vedantism, Confucianism, and Islamic Sufi Religious poetry."[54] However, Emerson, like all his fellow transcendentalists, was highly eclectic in his selection of elements from each body of thought. Further, he incorporated into his personal version of transcendentalism only those parts which were most congenial to his optimistic but rather austere temperament. He ignored the latent pessimism in the Hindu belief in the transmigration of souls, the pragmatic earth-bound origin of the ethics of Confucianism, the mutual incompatibility of the Hindu concept of karma and the Muslim concept of Kismat and the erotic symbolism pervading much of Sufi religious poetry. Of the three Oriental influences cited by Christ, the most important for Emerson was Vedantic mysticism. In Emerson's mind "a meeting of East and West" took place which was of historic importance. He introduced the Eastern thought to the Western mind and assimilated it in his writings and thinking.

Emerson was deeply influenced by Indian thought and wisdom. F.I. Carpenter remarks: "To Emerson's mind Hindu philosophy expressed the essence of orientalism. Often he identified the whole Orient with it. When speaking vaguely of Asia, he was usually thinking of Hindustan."[55] Essentially, his temperament was that of a Hindu, a fact many Hindu scholars have accepted.

Pratap Chunder Mazoomdar calls Emerson "the best Brahman."[56] He remarks: "Amidst this ceaseless, sleepless din and clash of Western materialism, this heart and restless energy, the character of Emerson shines upon India serene as the evening star. He seems to some of us to have been a geographical mistake. Perhaps Hindoos were closer kinsmen to him than his own nation because every typical Hindoo is a child of Nature."[57] Emerson himself had felt this spiritual inclination and affinity towards the Hindoos. Throughout his writings, he admitted his indebtedness to Indian thought in unambiguous terms.

Emerson looked Eastward in his early years. The year 1820 may well be regarded as the beginning of his interest in the Orient. He was introduced to Orientalism by his loving aunt Mary Moody Emerson who sent him, "A Hymn to Narayana"[58] by Sir William Jones. He was so deeply impressed by it that he copied a portion of the poem in his diary, a fact which shows his early interest in Orientalism. After reading this, he wrote back to his aunt on June 10, 1822: "I am curious to read your Hindu mythologies . . . all the books of knowledge, and all the wisdom of Europe twice told, like hidden in the treasure so the Brahmins."[59] During the next decade or so, Emerson's interest in Orientalism grew steadily and became more sharply defined. He read a large number of extracts including excerpts from the *Mahabharata* from various Indian philosophical books. According to Man Mohan Singh, he read about nineteen articles on India published in *Edinburgh Review* during the period 1821.[60] In the year 1836, he read William Jones's translation of the *Code of Manu*. Emerson had no knowledge of Sanskrit. For his reading, therefore, he had to depend on whatever English translations were available then. The English translations of Indian texts were mostly made by the efforts of the Asiatic Society of Bengal, and the translators of these texts were such persons as Sir William Jones, Henry Thomas Colebroke, Sir Charles Wilkins, Horace Hayman Wilson and Brain Houghton Hudgoson. In the *Journals* of 1838, he recorded that he had read and assimilated the essence of oriental works, namely, *The Laws of Manu*, "Buddha," "Confucius,"

"Zoroaster," Sir William Jones's translations of Asiatic poetry and the *Bhagvad Gita* which he first mistook for a Buddhist scripture, and Vishnu Sarma's *Heetopades*. Of all, the greatest single influence on Emerson was the *Bhagvad Gita*. He wrote: "I owed . . . my friend and I, . . . owed a magnificent day to the *Bhagvad Gita*. It was the first of books; it was as if an empire spoke to us, nothing small or unworthy but large, serene, consistent, the voice of an old intelligence which in another age and climate had pondered and thus disposed of the same question which exercise us." (*Journals*, VII, 511) It is observed that Emerson conceived he central concept of his philosophy, the concept of Over-Soul, in all probability, after reading the *Gita*, wherein the Supreme Spirit is called *Paramatman*.

For Emerson, Indian philosophy expressed the epitome of Orientalism. India was always mysterious and fascinating. He recorded in his *Journals*: "I cannot read a sentence in the book of the Hindoos without being elevated as upon the table land of the Ghats. It was such a rhythm as the winds of desert, such a tide as the Ganges, and seems as superior to criticism as the Himmaleh mounts." (*Journals*, I, 266) About the Vedas, he was so overjoyed that he wrote: "One wise sentence [from Vedas] is worth the state of Massachusetts many times over." (II, 24) This amply proves his spontaneous reaction, deep interest and fascination of the Orient. The long years of his studying of Indian philosophy and literature shaped and moulded his thought and philosophy, which ultimately led him to disband all authority and tradition. All his questions and doubts were peacefully and happily resolved; and his vacillating mind of self-reliance got confirmed in the Hindu thought. His philosophy and many of his basic doctrines were formed, not in ignorance, but fair knowledge of Hindu philosophy. His concept of God as the "Over-Soul," an impersonal and disinterested spirit who is manifest in Nature and whose laws transcend the realm of human good and evil is identical to the formless, all-pervading, beneficent supreme "Brahman" of the Upanishads.

Like the concept of Impersonal God, the concept of "Maya" or illusion has influenced Emerson a great deal. He equated Maya with the Platonic doctrine of the flux of things or variety and remarked that "the Hindoos, in their sacred writings, express the liveliest feelings, both of the essential identity and of that illusion which they conceive variety to be."[61] "Maya" means that Brahman is the ultimate reality and the phenomenal world is not ultimately real; in other words, has no *paramarthika satta.* Emerson in two of his poems "Illusion" and "Maya" hinted at the above Hindu concept. In 1861, he wrote in his *Journals* about the Maya of Vishnu. (IX, 302) In another context, he said that the world is born of Maya. (*Journals*, X, 159) The poem "Hamatreya" also seems to have been influenced by the concept of Maya where the difference between "I and You" or "Mine and You" has been regarded as ignorance.[62]

There is a similarity between the doctrine of Karma and Emerson's "Compensation." Fate, truly understood, is the effect of past karma (action) which must happen. Emerson accepts the law of Karma in general but does not seem to accept the deterministic aspect of it. This kind of disagreement suggests that he had properly understood the concept. He wrote in one of his *Journals*: "so long as I am weak, I shall talk of Fate, whenever the God fills me with his fullness, I shall see the disappearance of fate."[63] Though Emerson's support of Law of Karma has been criticized for its anti-Christian stance, Emerson always understood the simple logic involved in the law that "whatever you sow, so shall your reap." The Upanishads assert that all human sufferings have their origin in *Prarbdha Karma*, which means deeds of one's past life.

The doctrine of rebirth is a natural corollary to the law of Karma and an important Hindu and Buddhist concept. It implies that man will undergo a series of reincarnations, rebirths according to his desires. These constitute a vicious cycle which can be broken by realizing Ultimate Reality. This is known as liberation in Buddhism, and Moksha in Hinduism. The idea of rebirth or reincarnation is found throughout Emerson's works and journals. He wrote: "The transmigration of souls is no fable."[64] This doctrine, though antithetical to Christianity, has appealed to Emerson because it countered the notion of finality inherent in Christianity.

Many of Emerson's ideas and his basic beliefs like the primacy of the individual, the need for self-reliance, the relative unimportance of material welfare and the transient problems of the world, and the paramount importance of the formation of character and spiritual progress are found in the Indian scriptures. It is evident that his unswerving faith in the Supreme Reality, strong individualism and self-reliance were a part of legacy of his native Puritanism, and that it was further fortified by his study of Platonism and especially Neo-Platonism, European Romanticism, and Hindu philosophy, and made him emphasize self-reform in preference to institutional reform and organized philanthropy. He declared, "let every man shovel out his own snow, and the whole city will be passable." (*Journals*, V, 437)

Significantly enough, most of Emerson's ideas and doctrines suggest that he was deeply ecstatic of Indian literature and philosophy. His transcendentalism was strengthened by accepting various ideas from different cultures and philosophers. Of the ideas that enriched and enlivened his philosophy, the philosophical and religious ideas of ancient India form the most prominent, without which Emerson's transcendentalism would not have sustained its vitality, vigour, strength and beauty.

NOTES

1. Oliver Wendell Holmes, *Ralph Waldo Emerson* (Boston, 1884), p. 13.
2. Edward Waldo Emerson, *Emerson in Concord* (Boston, 1889), p. 9.
3. *Works* (Centenary Edition), Vol. X, p. 593.
4. *Ibid.*, p. 376.
5. Cabot, *A Memoir of Ralph Waldo Emerson* (Boston, 1887), p. 9.
6. *Emerson in Concord*, p. 9.
7. *Works*, Vol. V, p. 337.
8. James Eliot Cabot, *A Memoir of Ralph Waldo Emerson*, p. 478.

9. *Emerson in Concord*, p. 39.
10. *A Memoir of Ralph Waldo Emerson*, p. 59.
11. *Works*, VI, p. 137.
12. *A Memoir of Ralph Waldo Emerson*, p. 58.
13. Bacon and Berkley "have been friends to me," G.E. Woodberry, *Talks with Ralph Waldo Emerson*, p. 26.
14. On Augustine and Thomas Aquinas, see *Works*, I, p. 414.
15. George Willis Cooke, *Ralph Waldo Emerson: His Life, Writings and Philosophy* (Boston, 1881), p. 22.
16. Miss Peabody, *Reminiscences*, p. 371.
17. Sanborn, *The Personality of Emerson* (Boston, 1903), p. 40.
18. Qtd. Ralph L. Rusk, *The Life of Ralph Waldo Emerson* (New York, 1949), p. 507.
19. J.B. Moore, *Thoreau Rejects Emerson*, p. 241.
20. Qtd. H.R. Warfel, "Margaret Fuller and R.W. Emerson," *PMLA*, L. 576-94 (June 1935).
21. *Works*, III, p. 22.
22. *A Memoir of Ralph Waldo Emerson*, iii.
23. *Ibid.*, p. 295; and see also *Works*, XII, p. 48.
24. *Works*, III, p. 55; also see *The Selected Writings of Ralph Waldo Emerson*, p. 348.
25. Brooks Atkinson, ed., *The Selected Writings of Ralph Waldo Emerson* (New York, 1968), p. 49.
26. *Ibid.*, p. 49.
27. *Ibid.*, p. 50.
28. *The Growth of American Thought*, p. 304.
29. *Works*, V, p. 330.
30. *A Memoir of Ralph Waldo Emerson*, p. 161.
31. *Works*, V, p. 21 and p. 279; See also *Works*, XII, p. 225.
32. *Works*, V, p. 282.
33. *Ibid.*, XII, p. 227.
34. *Ibid.*, XII, p. 187 (from the *Dial*).
35. Qtd. Hartwig, "An Immortal Friendship," *Hibbert Journal* XXXVII, 102-14 (Oct. 1939).
36. *Ibid.*
37. See *The Correspondence of Carlyle and Emerson, 1834-72*, ed. C.E. Norton (Boston, 1888). The story of this friendship has been told brilliantly by Townsed Scudder, *The Lonely Wayfaring Man Emerson and Some English Men* (New York, 1936); also in brief

outline, by G.H. Harting, "An Immortal Friendship," *Hibbert Journal*, pp.102-14 (Oct. 1939).

38. *Emerson in Concord*, p. 36.
39. *A Memoir of Ralph Waldo Emerson*, p. 139.
40. C.E. Norton, ed. *Carlyle-Emerson Correspondence* (Boston, 1888) p. 311.
41. *Ibid.*
42. *The Reign of Wonder: Naivety and Reality in American Literature* (New York, 1967), p. 9.
43. Qtd. Ralph L. Rusk, *The Life of Ralph Waldo Emerson*, p. 507.
44. F.I. Carpenter, *Emerson Handbook* (New York, 1953), p. 214.
45. *The Complete Essays and Other Writings of Ralph Waldo Emerson*, p. 472 from "Plato or the Philosopher."
46. *Works*, IV, p. 54.
47. *Emerson and Asia* (New York, 1953), pp. 69-70.
48. M.S. Turpe, "A Quaker Source for Emerson's Sermon on the Lord's Supper," *The New England Quarterly*, XVII (March 1944) pp. 95-101.
49. David G. Harkins, *Ralph Waldo Emerson: His Maternal Ancestors with Some Reminiscences of Him* (Boston, 1886), p. 48.
50. *Complete Works of Ralph Waldo Emerson*, Vol. I, p. 10, "Nature."
51. P.R. Quin, "Emerson and Mysticism," *American Literature*, XXI (Jan. 1950), p. 399.
52. Leyla Goren, "Elements of Brahminism in Transcendentalism of Emerson," *The Emerson Society Quarterly*, 34 (I qtr. 1964), p. 8.
53. Arthur E. Christy, *The Orient in American Transcendentalism: A Study of Emerson, Thoreau, and Alcott* (New York, 1963), p. 266.
54. *Ibid.*, Chapters XI-XII.
55. *Emerson and Asia*, p. 103.
56. Pratap Chunder Mazoomdar, "Emerson as Seen from India," *Concord Harvest*, ed. K.W. Cameron (Hartford: Transcendental Books, 1970), p. 187.
57. *Ibid.*, p. 186.
58. Sir William Jones, trans. "A Hymn to Narayana" *American Transcendental Quarterly*, I, No. 20 (Fall 1973), pp. 578-83.
59. Ralph L. Rusk, ed. *The Letters of Ralph Waldo Emerson* (1939; rpt. New York and London: Columbia University Press, 1966), I, pp. 116-117.
60. Man Mohan Singh, *Emerson and India*, Diss. University of Pennsylvania, 1946.

61. *Works*, VI, p. 324.
62. *Complete Works*, IX, p. 36, "Hamatreya."
63. *Journals*, VI, p. 189; See also p. 317; Vol. VII, p. 8.
64. *Complete Works*, Vol. II, p. 32. "History."

Chapter III

Emerson and Vedanta

Emerson studied the sacred books of the East. Most of his ideas have found parallels in the Hindu philosophy. He articulated his experience of Many and One, the Individual Soul and the World Soul, the temporary and the everlasting, the moral laws and the spiritual laws, the good and the evil, the illusion and the reality. He regarded poetry and essays as the best media for communicating his experiences to the readers. Having recognized his profundity and depth, many of his contemporaries and the later critics called him a philosopher. He was essentially "a man of wisdom,"[1] and "the sage of Concord."[2] "A gifted visionary," a "seer" as William James reverently suggested. "A puritanical mystic with a poetic fancy and a gift for observation and epigram,"[3] as George Santayana called him. Robert Frost called him "a philosophical poet."[4]

Emerson's transcendental philosophy has, in many respects, a close resemblance to that of Vedanta. As a transcendentalist, he encouraged individualism, self-reliance, the innate goodness of man and rejected an exclusive intellectual approach to life. Monism, optimism, denial of evil which derived from Vedanta philosophy deeply influenced his view as well as his way of life. Carpenter writes: "His reading of Indian literature forms one of the most important chapters in the story of his literary development; for not only did he owe his poems 'Brahma' and 'Hamatreya' entirely to Hindu works but large parts of his essays on 'Plato', 'Fate', 'Illusions' and 'Immortality' are based on Hindu thought, and his famous 'Sphinx' probably shares in it."[5] Bliss Perry noticed "innate mystical tendencies" in Emerson. He observed: "He discovered in the Hindu writings, as he had already found in Neo-Platonism a reinforcement of certain natural tendencies in himself."[6]

Indian tradition is fundamentally religious, mystical and spiritual. It has always been identified with the Vedic tradition which dates back 5000 years. The scriptures of Vedic tradition are called *Shrutis* because they are revealed truths. They are the inner experiences of the Vedic *rishis* (the seers). They are said to have "timeless finality" *(nityatva)*. The Vedas (*samhitas*, *Brahmanas*, *Aranyakas* and *Upanishad*) are the *Shruti* texts. *Vedas* are "the earliest documents of the human mind,"[7] "the earliest record of the Indo-European race."[8]

The *Vedanta* literature, brief summaries in the *Vedas*, stands out as the most significantly "native philosophy of India."[9] It has attracted the great intellectuals of the West. Its influence on world thought has been very deep and widespread. Vedanta has influenced Schopenhauer, Hartman, Nietzsche, and Keyserling in Europe. Its influence on the Irish Renaissance is seen in the life and works of W.B. Yeats and G.W. Russel. Its great influence on American Transcendentalists is most vigorous and everlasting.

Schlegal observed: "Even the loftiest philosophy of the Europeans, the idealism of reason as set forth by the Greek philosophers, appears—in companion with the abundant life and vigour of Oriental idealism—like a feeble promethean spark against the full flood of sunlight. What distinguishes the *Vedanta* from all other philosophies is that it is at once religion and philosophy. In India, the two are inseparable."[10] The French historian, Victor Cousin, said: "When we read with attention the poetical and philosophical moments of the orient—above all, those of India we discover there many a truth so profound . . . that we are constrained to bend the knee before the philosophy of the East, and to see in this cradle of the human race the native land of the highest philosophy."[11]

The 'Veda' is derived from the Aryan root 'Vid' which means 'seeing' or 'to know'. It is seeing with mind's eye or intuitive seeing.[12] The knowledge derived from intuition was handed down from one generation to another by careful oral tradition to be compiled only about 1500 B.C.[13] The four *Vedas* are: *Rgveda, Yajurveda, Samaveda* and *Atharvaveda.* Each of these contains four parts: Hymns (*samhitas*), Ritual texts (*Brahmanas*), Forest Treatises (*Aranyakas*) and Teachings of sages (*Upanishads).* The Hymns were sung in praise of those deities who were worshipped and to whom sacrifices were done. The Ritual Texts also contained Hymns and were recited. Their directives were observed. The Forest Treatises contain the reflections of people retiring to the forests. The *Upanishads* are those treatises which contain the teachings of sages about the nature of the soul, the spirit, the world, and the Supreme Being.

The later Vedic period mainly consists of the philosophy of the *Upanishads*. *Upanishads* are the end part of *Vedas*. The root meaning of the word *Upanishad* may be grasped by splitting it into three: *Upa* means near, *ni* with certainty, *shad* destroy, go reach or attain. The word *Upanishad* stands for "the sitting down of the disciple near the teacher in a devoted manner to receive instruction about the highest Reality which loosens all doubts and destroys all ignorance of the disciple. Gradually the word came to signify any secret teaching about Reality and it is used by the *Upanishads* in this sense."[14] The *Upanishads* contain the essence of the speculative knowledge of the Veda and are therefore called the Vedanta, or the end of the Vedas. The *Upanishada* are many and, like the Vedas, were not composed at the same time or place or by the same person. And sometimes their teachings appear to be conflicting. They have, therefore, to be interpreted in a right way. The different interpretations have in course of time introduced different systems of philosophy. Thus, the *Upanishad*s became the basis for different philosophies,[15] each of which became a kind of school or tradition.

The *Upanishads* reveal the most sublime truths of Indian philosophy and the highest values of spiritual life. The persistent problems of metaphysics, ethics and religion are clearly set forth in the *Upanishads.* They are the source and substance of all *vedantic darsanas*, systems of philosophy. They deal with the two fundamental themes, the nature of Ultimate Reality, that is known as Brahman and the Atman, their interrelationship. According to the *upanishads* there is one Reality which is ultimate and final, above the relativity and absoluteness. This Reality is identified as Brahman, which is impersonal in character, said to be omnipresent, omnipotent, omniscient, all-pervading, infinitely great and infinitely small. It is viewed as an Eternity without beginning, middle and end. It is independent of all existence, both past and future, and Lord of all, at whose feet time rolls along.

It is the *Upanishads* that lead a man from ignorance to wisdom and from misery to eternal happiness. It is in Vedanta that theoretical speculation and practical spiritual experience go together. He who knows Brahman attains, as the *Taitirya Upanishad* affirms, the highest end of life. This sums up the wisdom of Vedanta and it means that Brahman, the metaphysical ground of all being, is also the goal of all moral and spiritual endeavours. The *mumuksa* or seeker after Brahman not only thinks reality, but also lives in it and realizes it. Then, all his doubts are resolved, and he lives in eternal peace and bliss. He becomes *Jnani*, and he communicates his *jnana* to others and in this manner, the tradition of *Upanishads* is maintained with unbroken continuity.

There are twelve *Upanishads* considered to be canonical or principal. They are: the *Isa*, the *Katha*, the *Taitriya*, the *Brhadarnyaka*, the *Svetasvara*, the *Prasna*, the *Mundaka*, the *Mandukya*, the *Aitreya*, the *Kausitaki*, the *Chandogya* and the *Kena.* Of these twelve, the first five belong to the *Yajurveda*, the next three to the *Atharva Veda*, the next two to the *Rg Veda* and the last two to the *Sama Veda*. The *Katha Upanishad* begins with the immortal discourse between Yama, the god of Death, the young Nachiketas, and teaches sublime ethical truths like self-reverence and self-sovereignty. The *Taitriya* contains the famous story of Bhrigu obtaining the mystic knowledge of Brahman as supremely blissful. In the *Brhadaranyaka Upanishad*, Yajnavalkya explains to his wife the nature of the immortal self, defines Brahman as the Inner Ruler of all beings and gives a psychological account of the three states of consciousness. The *Chandogya Upanishad* provides the largest number of topics or *Vishyaa Vakyas* for exposition in the *Vedanta Sutras*, of which the chief are the *Sadvidya* dealing with Brahman as the *sat*, the *Bhumavidya* defining the nature of Brahman as the infinitely blissful and *Daharavidya* which teaches the in-dwelling of Brahman in the hearts of all beings. The *Isavasya Upanishad* describes Atman as the Lord of the Universe and says that it moves and does not move, that it is near and far, and that it is inside everything and yet outside it. The *Kena Upanishad* raises the question about who it is that makes the mind, senses, speech, etc., active. It is the Atman. The senses and organs cannot work without the activation of the Atman. The *Mundaka Upanishad* distinguishes between two kinds of knowledge, the higher and the lower. By having the higher knowledge, we know everything. This is the knowledge of the Atman. This *Upanishad* employs the celebrated simile of two birds on the same tree to bring out the relation between the finite self and the Supreme Self. The *Mandukya Upanishad* is considered to be the most important. It explains how the same *atman* passes through the three states (*avasthas*): dream (*swapna)*, waking *(jugupsa)*, and deep sleep (*sushupta*). It can be realized in its original nature only in a state beyond deep sleep, which is known as *turiya.*

All the *Upanishads*, however, teach the same central truth, that Brahman is the source of the creation and the supreme end of life. The *mumuksa*, who seeks Brahman as the All-Self, sees Brahman intuitively, becomes a *mukta* and imparts his wisdom to others also who seek it. Upanishadic wisdom is not an esoteric doctrine meant for elect souls and monopolized by them, but is a rich spiritual treasure which is accessible to all who would undergo the necessary discipline. It is not secret but sacred in the sense that only the pure in heart can attain peace that passeth all understanding. The value of *Upanishads* does not lie in merely by-hearting slokas, but in living the Upanishadic life and realizing its importance.

Emerson derived so much from the *Upanishads* and the *Bhagvad Gita* that throughout his writings he admitted his indebtedness in unambiguous terms. In his *Journal*, he paid the following tribute to Vedic thought: "It is the sublime as heat and night end a breathless ocean. It contains every religious sentiment, all the grand ethics, which visit in turn each noble poetic mind. . . . It is of no use to put away the book; if I trust myself in the woods, or in a boat upon the pond, Nature makes a *Brahmin* of me presently: eternal compensation, unfathomable power, unbroken silence. . . . This is her creed. Peace, she said to me, and purity, and absolute abandonment—these panaceas expiate all sin and bring you to the beatitude of the Eight Gods."[16]

(i) *Paramatman* and Over-Soul

The first major contribution of Emerson to his basic Idealistic philosophy is the doctrine of Over-Soul which is parallel to the Hindu doctrine of *Paramatman*. The *Paramatman* is the Supreme Soul, which is one without second. According to the *Upanishads*, it is impersonal in character, the underlying principle of all existence. It is Brahman, the Ultimate Reality or Self, the Unseen One, which holds the infinite universe together. It is not a combination of unrelated fragments; it sees all things as parts of a great whole and it tries to bind all these parts together in that whole. In the *Kena Upanishad* (I: 2, 3, 4, 5, 6, 7, & 8) it is defined as "the ear of the ear, the mind of the mind, the speech of the speech, the life of the life, the eye of the eye. That which cannot be thought by mind, but by which mind is able to think; that which is not seen by the eye, but by which the eye is able to see; that which cannot be heard by the ear, but by which the ear is able to hear."

Sankara, the great Advaitin, has beautifully extolled Brahman in his interpretations of *Sutras* and *Upanishads*. He used "remorseless logic" in order to show that all the scriptures agree in holding Brahman to be the only worth. He says: "All ideas of non-Brahman are but ignorance."[17] Commenting on *Brhadaranyaka Upanishad*, Sankara says, "there is no plurality whatsoever in it. Brahman the object of realization."[18] "But there is not that second thing separate from it which it can see."[19]

Emerson's concept of Soul is similar. "We learn that the highest is present to the soul of man," writes Emerson in "Nature," that the dread universal essence, which is not wisdom, or love, or beauty, or power, but all in one and each entirely, is that for which all things exist, and by which they are."[20] In "Self-Reliance," he writes, "the resolution of all into the ever-blessed ONE."[21] In his essay "Over-Soul," the same idea is conveyed: "The Supreme Critic of the errors of the past and the present, and the only prophet of that which must be is that great nature in which we rest as the earth lies in the soft arms of the atmosphere; that Unity; that Over-Soul, within which everyman's particular being is contained and made one with all other."[22] The idea of Over-Soul is central to Emerson's philosophy. It is not a concept, when stripped of metaphor, is curiously featureless, sometimes "moral sentiment." But, it is the Over-Soul, the animating principle of Cosmos. He professes in his essay, "Over-Soul": "When it breathes through his [man's] intellect, it is genius; when it breathes through his will, is virtue; when it flows through his affection, it is love."[23]

A distinct change in the use of words may be noticed from "Nature" to "Over-Soul." In the initial stage, Emerson used "Holy-Ghost," "Spirit," "Mind," and "Reason" for the Supreme God. Gradually, this transition was shifted to the use of words like "Over-Soul," "Soul" and "Intuition"[24] in his later years; "Reason" in the sense of "Intuition," "Spirit" in the "Creator," "God" in the "Father." Finally, he succeeded in using "Over-Soul" which asserts: "We live in succession . . . universal as the rising of the wind."[25] This Over-Soul is the highest reality. In his essay "Experience," he states: "That nothing is of us or our works, that all is of God."[26] He further writes, "the simple infinity of the soul is the text and the rest is comment."[27] The thought is profound and intelligible, and the realization is deep when studied in the light of Hindu thought.

Emerson's Over-Soul is not a static, but an active, dynamic principle. Though it cannot be really seen through sense organs, its manifestation in nature is very much felt. He never hesitates to write: "The senses interfere everywhere, and mix their own structure with all they report of." (*Journals*, VI, 295) "Souls never touch their objects. . . . Dream delivers us to dream, and there is no end to illusion . . . least we shall find reality." (*Journals*, VI, 52-53) If nature is illusion and its laws are permanent, the reality which imposes these laws is, Emerson writes: "It is the uniform effect of culture on the human mind, not to shake out faith in the stability of particular phenomena, as of heat, water, azote; but to lead us to regard nature as phenomenon, not substance; to attribute necessary existence to spirit; to esteem nature as an accident and an effect." (*Journals*, I, 54) He is never weary of restating: "On this power, this all dissolving unity, the emphasis of heaven and earth is laid. Nature is brute but as the soul quickens it; Nature always the effect, mind the flowing cause." (*Journals*, VIII, 212) Of what spirit or mind is nature the effect? Emerson answers: "True Intellect builds the Universe and is the key to all it contains." (*Journals*, XII, 214) "Every law in nature, as gravity, centripetence, repulsion, polarity, undulating, has a counterpart in the intellect." (*Journals*, VIII, 211) He argues that "man does not see that he only is real and the world is mirror and echo." (*Journals*, X, 185) "We have learned that we do not see directly, but mediately, and that we have no means of correcting these coloured and distorting lenses which we are, or of computing the amount of their errors." (*Journals*, III, 77) He calls the Appearance the World and "that God will teach a human mind, and so makes it the receiver of a certain number of congruent sensations, which we call sun and moon, man and woman, house and trade." (*Journals*, I, 52)

In his early years, Emerson solely depended on Christian tradition to clarify what god is. He accepted the scripture's authority that God is personal. He viewed Christ as simply a human being. In his "Divinity School of Address," he called Jesus, "the friend of man."[28] Without questioning, Emerson blindly believed that man lives in a God-centred universe, as professed in the Christian religion. Man is helpless and cannot comprehend and hence, he must totally surrender to the will of God. His God was personal. He did not give any rational justification to his views. Like a Puritan he drew enormous inspiration from the traditional explanations of Christianity. In his later years, he changed this perception. He opposed historical Christianity, because it was historical—because it spoke "as if God were dead."[29] He was convinced that "God is, not was; that he speaks; not spoke."[30] He never degraded any religious beliefs, although he had different views about the conception of God. He had always upheld the greatness and goodness in religion. "Christ preached the greatness of man," he wrote, "we preach the greatness of Christ. The first is affirmative, the last negative." (*Journals*, X, 186) According to him historical Christianity suffered from many deficiencies. The obnoxious exaggeration of Jesus as God to the extent of neglecting what he stood for, Emerson called the main defect of historical Christianity. He observed that Jesus is the only soul in history who has appreciated the worth of man. Jesus saw that God incarnates himself in man; he saw the mystery of the soul. But the doctrinal formulations of Christianity distorted the message of Jesus. Jesus had said, Emerson declared, "Would you see God, see me; or see thee, then thou also thinkest as I now think." But, in the next following ages, this was completely distorted. Jesus was misrepresented and misquoted. "Churches are not built on his principles," Emerson wrote, "but on his tropes. Christianity became a mythus." (*Journals*, I, 129) Thus, Emerson believed that "the exaggeration of the personal, the positive, the ritual," "corrupts all attempts to communicate religion." (*Journals*, I, 134)

For Emerson God is not personal; not relatively real but absolute reality; the Vedic Impersonal. "God is not a relation or a part," he wrote, "but the whole." (*Journals*, II, 121) His God has no attributes, is featureless; "Is not man in our day described by the very attributes which once he gave to his God? Is not the sea his minister; the clouds his chariot; the flame his wheels; and the winds his wings?" (*Journals*, III, 324-25) He questioned the very existence of God in personal form. "I deny personality to God," he wrote, "because it is too little, not too much." (*Journals*, IV, 416) "Is God a person? No," (*Journals*, IV, 186) he denied emphatically. He observed: "I feel that there is some profanation in saying He is personal. To represent him as an individual is to shut him out of my consciousness." (*Journals*, IV, 404) For his views, Emerson was criticized, denigrated and attacked by his contemporary clergymen, critics and scholars. He was accused of blasphemy. He was branded as an atheist, a pantheist. But Emerson never reacted seriously or violently against any such charges; he maintained distinct Oriental calm. He unsettled the foundation of morality, abolished the distinction between right and wrong, and reduced personality to a mask. He stated that an understood God is not God at all. Frothingham observed that "the personal God of the Theist he will not accept, for He is too much like a man."[31] Further, he said, "he neither dogmatises nor deifies. On the contrary, his chief anxiety seems to be to avoid committing himself to opinion; to keep all questions open; to close no avenue in any direction to the free ingress and egress of the mind."[32]

God for Emerson is impersonal. This Impersonal element has been clearly emphasized in the *Upanishads*. The impersonal character of God is repeatedly mentioned in various *Upanishads*. In the *Katha Upanishad*, in the form of a story through the dialogue between Yama, the god of death, and Nachiketa, the impersonal character of God is beautifully described. To the boy's persistent questioning, Yama answers that the *Atman* is the ultimate truth. But it is smaller than the smallest and yet greater than the greatest. It is imperishable, it has no birth and death. In truth, there is no death for the "I." Brahman can be described only *neti, neti*, it is not this, it is not this. The *Katha Upanishad* (III.15) described: "That which is inaudible, intangible, indivisible, indestructible, which cannot be tested, nor smelt, eternal, without beginning or end, greater than the great (*mahat*), the fixed. He who knows it is released from the jaws of death."[33] We find it directly stated in *Brahadaranyaka Upanishad* (IV.iv.25): "Verily, that great unborn Soul undecaying, undying, immortal, fearless, is Brahman."[34] The *Mundaka Upanishad* (IV.iv.25) states: "Him (i.e. Brahma) alone knows as the only Soul (*Atman*). Other words dismiss."[35] The *Svetasvatara Upanishad* (I.16) points: "The Soul (*Atman*) which pervades all things . . . this is Brahma."[36] In *Brahadaranyaka Upanishad* (III.viii.2), the nature of *Atman* is perhaps more clearly stated: "It is not large, and not minute; not short, not long; without blood, without fat; without shadow, without darkness; without wind, without ether; not adhesive, not tangible; without smell, without taste; without eyes, ears, voice or mind, without heart, breath, or mouth; without personal or family name; unaging, undying, without fear, immortal, dustless, not uncovered or covered; without nothing before, nothing behind, nothing within. It consumes no one and is consumed by no one. It is the unseen seer, the unheard hearer, the unthought thinker, the unknown knower. There is no other seer, no other hearer, no other thinker, no other knower. That is the Eternal in which (*akasha*) is woven and which is interwoven with it."[37]

"Brahma" (1857) is extraordinary in the sense that it expresses the Oriental counterpart of the Platonic idea of "unity in variety," and it is common to all mystical separation. The uniqueness of the poem lies in its adoption of the point of view of God, and of God conceived as the impersonal creative energy of the universe. The opening stanza is almost identical to the passage from the *Vishnu Purana* that Emerson copied in his Journal in 1845. (*Journals*, IX, 34)

> If the red slayer think he slays,
> Or if the slain think he is slain,
> They know not well the subtle ways,
> I keep, and pass, and turn again.[38]

It also paraphrases the *Bhagvad Gita*:

> He who considers this Self as a slayer
> Or he who thinks that this Self is slain

Neither of these knows the Truth
For it does not slay, nor is it slain.39

The same idea is expressed in his essay on "Plato" (1850): "The same, the same; friend and foe are one stuff; the ploughman, the plough and the furrow are of one stuff; and the stuff is such and so much that the variations of form are unimportant."[40] The poem embodies the concept of impersonal God and the unity of God. The distinct philosophy of Vedanta is summed up in the last stanza of the poem:

They reckon ill who leave me out;
When me they fly, I am the wings;
I am the doubter and the doubt
And I the hymn the Brahmin sings.[41]

"Each and All" (1839) illustrates the idea of "unity in variety." According to Emerson, there is perfect harmony and beauty in Nature. "All are needed by each one; Nothing is fair or good alone."[42] (ll.11-12). The same idea is conveyed in his essay "Nature": "Although the works of nature are innumerable and all different, the result or the expression of them all is similar and single. Nature is a sea of forms radically alike and even unique."[43] Each thing is beautiful, if seen in its proper place in relevance to the whole. "Nothing is beautiful alone; nothing but is beautiful in the whole."[44] Emerson captures the beauty of the whole nature in the last lines:

Again I saw, again I heard,
The rolling river, the morning bird,
Beauty through my senses stole.[45] (ll. 44-49)

Again in his most complex and paradoxical poem, "The Sphinx" (1841), Emerson expresses the cosmic unity. Thoreau rightly responded to the poem and wrote in his *Journal* that the Sphinx was "man's insatiable and questioning spirit." (I, 229) The Sphinx comments on the reposeful harmony in nature, a harmony of peace, love, balance, serenity. Only man, the Sphinx announces:

crouches and blushes,
Absconds and conceals;
He creepeth and peepth,
He patters and steals;
Infirm, melancholy,
Jealous glancing around,
An oaf, an accomplice,
He poisons the ground.[46] (ll. 49-56)

The last five stanzas present an account of man's seeking, struggling and rejecting. To the Sphinx's original question: "why is man out of tune with the harmony of all other things?" the poet speaking for man answers that the infinite diversity and complexity of the world are bound by the greater unity of a whole that expresses itself in all the parts. So, Sphinx, Nature and Man are all parts of a perpetually and dynamically pulsating All.

Like the Vedic seers, Emerson had never accepted the phenomenal God. His conception of God has no form or shape. He observed: "The things that are seen are temporal; the things that are unseen, are eternal."[47] Emerson does not deny the existence of matter, but it is less real than the soul, the ideal reality. Nature, according to him, is infinitised finite as it were. Behind the phenomenal world there lies the infinite law, the absolute, which is formless and shapeless. "It always speaks of the Spirit. It suggests the absolute. It is a perpetual effect. It is a great shadow pointing always to the sun behind us."[48] This Law is all-pervasive. It lies "at the centre of nature and radiates to the circumference."[49] It has to be respected by man. "Any distrust of the permanence of laws would paralyse the faculties of man."[50] This law "holds true throughout nature. So intimate is this unity, that, it is easily seen, it lies under the undermost garment of Nature, and betrays its service in Universal Spirit."[51] Man must discover this law that is hidden in the creation. Every philosophy must aim at its discovery. This discovery is enlightenment, knowledge and bliss. This will emancipate man. Emerson writes: "We can see God in the coarse, and as it were, distinct phenomena of the matter; but when we try to define and describe himself, both language and thought desert us, and we are as helpless as forts and savages."[52] Emerson nowhere mentions that nature should be worshipped as God. This again, he implies, becomes personalized. But he states that through nature "man has access to the entire mind of the Creator, is himself the Creator in the finite."[53] Emerson's God is therefore not Nature but is all-pervading omnipresent, both immanent and transcendent. "And what is God?" asked Emerson and himself thus answered: "We cannot say, but we see clearly enough. We cannot say, because he is the unspeakable, the immeasurable, the perfect; but we see plain enough in what direction it lies. First, we see plainly that the All is in man." (*Journals*, IV, 127) Emerson's creating spirit which is one with the Over-Soul, is all-pervasive, and is synonymous with the Supreme Being, which he has not named.[54] This Supreme Being is identified with the Brahman of the *Upanishads*. Emerson himself testified to his reading of the Hindu writings and their fundamental Unity. "The rapture of prayer and ecstasy of devotion lose all being in one Being. This tendency finds its highest expression in the religious writings of the past, and chiefly in the Indian scriptures, in the *Vedas*, the *Bhagvad Gita*, and the *Vishnu Purana*."[55]

In the *Vedas*, we find a clear distinction between man's 'self' and the Over-Soul, the *jivatman* and *paramatman*, the individual self and the Supreme Self; or between the apparent man and the real man. In the *Mundaka Upanishad* (I.i.4), the two kinds of knowledge, the higher and the lower are distinguished. "There are two knowledges to be known—as indeed the knower of Brahma are wont to say: a higher (*para)* and also a lower (*apara*)."[56] The higher is that whereby that Imperishable (*akshara*) is apprehended. It is again stated: "That which is indivisible, ungraspable, without family, without caste, without sight or hearing is It, without hand or foot, Eternal, all-pervading, omnipresent, exceedingly subtle; that is the Imperishable, which the wise perceive as the source of Beings."[57] (*Mundaka Upanishad*, I.i.6). The relationship between the Imperishable and the perishable is mentioned in the same Upanishad (I.i.7) as follows: "As a spider emits and draws in [its thread], as herbs arise on the earth, as the hairs of the head and body from a living person, so from the Imperishable arises everything here."[58] Thus, man's 'self' is lower, while the 'Self' is higher. But, the higher Self is hidden and concealed in the lower self. The lower 'self' is the reflection of the Higher; but the reflection cannot exist without the object reflected; so man must know this higher 'Self'. The search must be made by every individual for himself, there is not one who can help revealing the 'Self'. This is hidden mystery.

Emerson extols the relationship between the individual and the all-pervasive Over-Soul. His philosophy teaches how this absolute, Impersonal Spirit is concealed in human soul. The individual soul, according to him, does not exist apart from the Absolute because "God is the substratum of all souls." (*Journals*, II, 323) Therefore, "the purpose of this life seems to be to acquaint a man with himself. He is not to live to the future as described to him, but to live to the real future by living to the real present. The highest revelation is that God is in every man." (*Journals*, III, 201) Emerson is emphatic about this unity because as long as the soul seeks God from without, it can never have peace and happiness. But, when it sees the "Great God" far within its own nature, "then it sees that always itself is a party to all that can be, that always it will be informed of that which will happen, and therefore, it is pervaded with great peace." (*Journals*, IV, 121) The unity achieved within should be the first step in endeavour towards perfection. "The reason why the world lacks unity, and lies broken and in heaps, is because man is disunited with himself."[59] When the soul in man expresses itself and unites with the Higher Self, it becomes dominating principle in life. Such a soul becomes one with the whole existence. There is no division or distinction. His actions become purified and real since he attributes everything to the divine principle. He is a man of integrity and perfection. His actions are not his own but guided by a spiritual impulse, the instinct of the soul. No human laws can bind him. He is Truth itself.

True Religion is man's self-conscious attempt to rediscover himself, reestablish his lost relations with the Cosmos and restore shattered harmony and peace. The way of Hinduism is inward and not outward seeking. All other religions except Buddhism and Hinduism follow the outward way, hence they have miserably failed to free man from misery and sorrow. Where all religions fail, the *Upanishads* upon which the whole Hinduism is built succeeds. It is stated in the *Katha Upanishad* (II.ii.1): "A rare discriminating man, desiring immortality, turns his eyes away [from sense objects], and then sees the indwelling self."[60] Sankara says that the indwelling self is one's own reality. Emerson follows a similar path. His call was "return to the unbounded souls of the world."[61] To such a man who achieves unity, "this bitterness of His and mine ceases."[62] In conformity with the views of Plotinus and Prochus, Emerson writes in his *Journal*: "The purified soul bears nothing." (*Journals*, VII, 310)

According to Emerson, God cannot be realized through sense organs, which are limited and finite. The senses must be transcended in order to perceive the Spirit. When the inner self begins to dominate the outer mechanism, the object steadily surrenders to the higher force and becomes one with the subject. Emerson lays strong emphasis on the obedience of the senses to the soul. He says, the insight must proceed from obedience. Through spiritual insight man can perceive the nature of the soul. He may well say at the end, I *am* God, or *aham Brahmasmi* (I *am* Brahman). Knowing God is not an intellectual acquirement, but an intuitional realization of one's true nature. Emerson wrote in his essay "The Over-Soul": "Ineffable is the union of man . . . the heart with his presence."[63] This approximated the Oriental depth and idealism.

The *Upanishads* point out that once one has rediscovered the inner potentialities, and established firm relationship with the Soul, one will be free from fear and sorrow. The *Isa Upanishad* (I.6) states: "Now, he who on all beings looks as just (*eva*) in the Self (*atman*), and on the Self as in all beings—he does not shrink away from Him."[64] "Then what delusion (*moha*), what sorrow (*soka*) is there of him who perceives the unity (*Isa Upanishad*, I.7)"[65]

The *Brahadaranyaka Upanishad* (I.iv.2 & 4) also reveals: "Verily fear arises from a second."[66] You have attained that which is free from fear, O Janaka."[67] The *Taitriya Upanishad* (II.vii) says: "For truly, when one finds fearlessness as a foundation in that which is invisible, bodiless (*an-atmya*), undefined, non-based, then he has reached fearlessness."[68] According to this *Upanishad*, the enlightened man after realizing the bliss of Brahman is not afraid of anything. Sankara says: "The *Atman* is one with Brahman; this is the highest truth, Brahman alone is real, there is none but He. When He is knower as the supreme reality, there is no other existence but Brahman."[69] In the same way, Emerson emphasizes that man has to realize that "his being is without bound."[70] He continues, "that by virtue of the power in him—call it soul, moral sentiment, genius, virtue, or Reason—man is not to be distinguished from the divine Essence." (*Journals*, III, 235) He observes: "Of the universal mind each individual man is one more incarnation."[71]. "God is around us and in us and the feeblest is yet divine."[72]

By identifying man with God, Emerson has posed a serious threat to the existence of religious and social institutions. Emerson viewed that any institution which makes man bow to its established views is dangerous. It is an anathema to freedom of conscience. It will not guarantee him spiritual freedom. He cannot discover the essence of spirit within himself. Emerson observed: "The doctrine of the divine nature being forgotten, a sickness infects and dwarfs the constitution. Once man was all; now he is an appendage, a nuisance. And because the indwelling Supreme Spirit cannot wholly be got rid of, the doctrine of it suffers this perversion, that the divine nature is attributed to one or two persons, and denied to all the rest, and denied with fury."[73] In the essay "Young American," he observed, in modern society man has lost his dignity in the brutish struggle for the survival of the fittest. He states: "Our condition is like that of the poor wolves, if one of the flock wound himself or so much as limp, the rest eat him up incontinently."[74]

Man is not merely a rational creature, but spiritual being. His life must be spiritual in order to attain peace and happiness in himself. Moral life for a spiritual being is a God-centred life. As man realizes God within himself, he will recognize the same in all beings. Such a man is endowed with love; he simply loves not only his fellow beings but also other creatures. No distinction stands in his way. "The height of culture, the highest behaviour," Emerson writes, "consists in the identification of the Ego with the universe; so that when a man says, I hope, I find, I think, he might properly say, the human race thinks or finds or hopes."[75] Man must work towards this realization, attending to the universal consciousness. "The eternal tendency of the soul is to become universal, to animate the last extremities of organisation." (*Journals*, IV, 287) The highest aim of life on the earth is the perfection of character. Emerson writes: "The whole object of the universe to us is the formation of character. If you think you came into being for the purpose of taking an important part in the administration of events, to guard a province of the moral creation from ruin, and that its salvation hangs on the success of your single arm, you have wholly mistaken your business." (*Journals*, II, 241) "Let a man learn to lose for the permanent in the mutable and fleeting; let him learn to bear the disappearance of things he was wont to reverence without losing his reverence; let him learn that he is here, not to work but to be worked upon; and that, though abyss upon under abyss, and opinion displace opinion, all are at last contained in the Eternal cause: 'If my bark sink, 'tis to another sea."[76]

Ultimately, Emerson says in concurrence with the Upanishads that man must rely on God for inspiration, freedom, vitality, peace, happiness and tiding over problems, anxiety and tensions. Relying on one's own self is relying on God. "The true happiness consists in self-reliance."[77] Self-reliance, according to Emerson, is "the height and perfection of God,"[78] and it is reliance on God. Life is full of struggles and pains. These may be overcome by relying on God within. Man, according to Emerson, is not a "Hero" or a demi-god of Carlyle, but a saint; not a doer but a thinker; not a static man but a dynamic man; not a dormant man but an active participant in life; not a pessimist but an optimist. The great man as Emerson views has the greatest soul force, strongest spiritual vision and highest perception of universal laws.

Emersion's great man is God-intoxicated man who is essentially a spiritual being. To be spiritual is the highest goal of life. "I count him a great man," Emerson wrote, "who inhabits a higher sphere of thought,"[79] "who is a man of 'honour', of 'taste' and 'humanity'."[80] His great man is a composition of several persons,[81] a more complete man,[82] pure from all pertness or egotism,[83] a sufficient man, an officer equal to his office,[84] exempt from envy,[85] or hatred (his time is worth too much),[86] of daring imagination,[87] has perception of universal laws (little minds are little through failure to see them),[88] impartial and universal[89] abides by the "eternal law of man and of the world."[90]

Emerson's great man completely "stands on God."[91] To him the entire world bows. The whole creation sings with him: it is a blissful state. He is held in high esteem; even gods revere him. Emerson's Over-Soul needs no shrines, no institutions no rituals, no prophets, no revelations but its own. Like the Hindu *Atman*, it is all in all—perfect, pure, self-revealing, luminous, omnipotent, infinite and transcendental. "The soul gives itself original, and pure," Emerson writes, "so come I to live in thoughts, and act with energies which are immortal."[92]

Emerson accepted the Vedantic concept of God. He admitted that God is all-pervading. Things may differ in nature. But they are the manifestation of the same God. He was impressed by Plato's expression, "God geomatrizes." (*Journals*, VII, 72) Emerson derived from Plotinus the doctrine of emanation and found confirmation in Indian scriptures. "I believe," he said, "in the omnipresence; that is, that the all is in each particle; that entire nature reappears in every leaf and moss." (*Journals*, IV, 84) He introduced the Eastern thought to the Western mind and he assimilated it fully in his writings. The historic dualism of East and West in Emerson's mind was closely related to the philosophic dualism of ideal and real. He wrote: "The unity of Asia and the detail of Europe; the infinitude of the Asiatic soul and the defining result-loving, machine-making, surface-seeking, opera-going, Europe—Plato came to join, and by contact to enhance the energy of each."[93] The mysticism of ancient East, the philosophic dualism of Plato, and the intense religious piety of Puritan past contributed characteristically to formulation of Emerson's ideas. As Pratap Chundar Mazoomdar maintains: "Emerson has all the wisdom and spirituality of the Brahman. Brahmanism is an acquirement, a state of being rather than a creed. In whomsoever the eternal Brahman breathed his unquenchable fire, he was the Brahman. And in that sense Emerson was the best of Brahman."[94] Another Indian scholar, Herambachandra Maitra wrote of the "modern spirit with the noblest teachings of ancient times."[95] The sage of Concord regarded himself as the American scholar and stimulated the mind of Americans and widened their horizons, by exploring the riches of Oriental literature.

(ii) **Maya and Illusion**

The ancient Vedic scriptures declare that the physical world operates under the fundamental law of *maya*, the principle of relativity, duality, inversion, contrast, oppositional states. God, the sole Life, is an Absolute Unity; He cannot appear as the separate and diverse manifestations of a creation except under a false or unreal dominance of *maya*. The ancient prophets were referring to *maya* when they spoke of Satan (literally in Hebrew, "the adversary"). The Greek Testament, as an equivalent for "Satin," uses *diabolus* or devil. The shadowy force or veil which hides the Eternal Verity is described thus by Christ: "The devil . . . abode not in the truth, because there is no truth in him. When he speaketh of his own: or he is a liar, and the father of it" (John viii.44). *Maya* is beginningless in the sense of its structural inherence in the phenomenal worlds—ever in transitional flux in antithesis to the Divine Immortality. "The devil sinneth *from the beginning*. For this purpose the Son of God was manifested, that he might destroy the works of the devil." (I John iii.8) That is to say: The manifestation of Christ consciousness within man's own being constitutes the sole escape from *maya*.

Every great scientific discovery of modern times has served as a confirmation of this simple pronouncement of the *rishis*. Newton's Law of Motion is a law of *maya*. According to him, to every action there is always an equal and contrary reaction; the mutual actions of any two bodies are always equal and oppositely directed. Action and reaction are thus exactly equal. Fundamental mutual activities all betray their exactly mayic origin. Electricity, for example, is a phenomenon of repulsion and attraction; its electrons and protons are electrical opposites. The entire phenomenal world is under the inexorable sway of polarity; no law of physics, chemistry, or any other science is ever found free from inherent opposite or contrasted principles. Nature herself is *maya*.

The view that the world is a reflection of ego, a mere appearance is found in the Vedantic philosophy. Philosophically, the idea is more important than conceiving the world as Brahman as it has been greatly misconstrued. Sankara says the world is a *Maya*. Many Western philosophers have corroborated the idea. Kant said that the world is only a phenomenon. Parmenides, Plato and Plotinus had said the same thing in different ways. The influence of these thinkers on Emerson in this regard has frequently been pointed out.[1] Emerson conceived the phenomenal ego as false and illusion and his idea has been closely identified with the Vedantic thought of *maya*.

The distinction between the phenomenal and the super phenomenal has been made quite clear in the Upanishadic thought. The phenomenal, though it appears to be real, is only fragment of its totality. Diversity and manifoldness are only an appearance. The *Chandogya Upanishad* (III. Xiv.1) states: "Verily everything is the Brahman."[2] This statement does not mean that everything, as we see it, is the Supreme Spirit itself, but that without the Supreme Spirit nothing, not even the worst, can have existence. The *Brihadaranyaka Upanishad* (IV. iv. 19) says: "There is on earth no diversity. He gets death after death who perceives here seeming diversity."[3] Also the *Chandogya Upanishad* (VII. xxvi.2) quotes: "The seer sees not death, nor sickness, nor any distress. The seer sees only the All, obtains the All entirely."[4] That is the real Brahma, the undifferentiated Unity. The lower Brahma of sense-manifoldness, in which everything appears as a self-subsistent entity, is merely an appearance due to a person's ignorance that all is essentially one; that is, it is an illusion. The *Maitri Upanishad* (VI.3) says plainly of the two Brahmas: "There are, assuredly, two forms of Brahma: the formed and the formless. Now, that which is the formed is unreal; that which is the formless is real."[5]

Maya is not illusion, but a peculiar power of God for creating the world. It has led to many misunderstandings. At first it meant the original, inexplicable power, or energy of the Supreme Spirit. It is the mysteriousness or inexplicability that was emphasized by the word. It did not mean the unreality of the world or that the world is merely Non-being.

Maya can be dealt and understood both from objective or metaphysical and subjective or epistemological points of view. From the objective side, *Maya* is attributable not so much to the knower, as to the One which hides his true nature. The Self, the Immortal One hides himself under the cover of name and form. "Life (*prana*) verily is the Immortal. Name and form are the real. By them that Life is veiled."[6] (*Brihadaranyaka Upanishad* I. iv. 3). Everything is enveloped by him as its inside and outside.[7] (*Brihadaranyaka Upanishad* II. V. 18). Brahman performs a supernatural trick in appearing as many. The whole world is thus subject to cosmic illusion: "This whole world the illusion-maker projects out of this (*Brahma*). And in it by illusion (*maya*) the other (the individual) is confined."[8] (*Svetasvatara Upanishad* IV. 9). From the subjective side, it is not the magic performed by Brahman, but the individual self's ignorance and persistence in the false belief that it is different from the real Self. In order to illustrate this, Sankara uses the stock similes of rope and snake, the distant post appearing like a man, the mirage and the like.

According to Sankara, the existence of "Self" is proved, which is the only reality. The knowing self, says Sankara, is not an object; objects are superimposed on it. The purpose of Vedanta is to free one's self from superimpositions, the cause of evil and wrong knowledge, and attain the unity of the Self. Self has a dual aspect—the empirical, phenomenal, changing, or apparent and the transcendental, eternal, changeless, or real. The phenomenal self is the individual self, the *antahnkarnah*, or the self that undergoes a series of experiences and suffers. It is identified with the body and mind and is characterized as the doer and experiencer. Whereas the *Atman* is a pure consciousness. "*Atman* is Brahman and Brahman is *Atman*"[9] (*Chandogya Upanishad*, V.xi.1). "In its light all this shines"[10] (*Katha Upanishad*, II.ii.15). "It is pure Being, being all-pervading and without constituent parts."[11] This is higher Self (the Pure Consciousness), characterized by being free from all evil, suffering and the like. This can be immediately known intuitively. That consciousness can be immediately apprehended without objectivity.

Emerson's doctrine of illusion is in complete agreement, with the Vedantic doctrine of *Maya*. He has derived immense inspiration from the Hindu scriptures. Corresponding to "I am Brahman"[12] (*Aham Brahmasmi*, *Brihadaranyaka Upanishad*, I.iv. 10). Emerson wrote: "Who shall define to me an individual? I behold with awe and delight many illustrations of the one Universal Mind. I see my being imbedded in it. As a plant in the earth so I grow in God. I am only a form of him. He is the soul of me. I can even with mountainous aspiring say, *I am God*, by transferring my Me out of the filmys & unclear precinct of my body, my fortunes, my private will." (*Journals*, V, 336-37) Both Sankara and Emerson believed that man in his inmost being is one with the non-dual Reality. "In all my lectures," Emerson declared: "I have taught one doctrine, namely, the infinitude of the private man." (*Journals*, V, 380) Not only is the soul of man open to the attributes of God, not only is God within him and 'about him' but "he is part of God himself." (*Journals*, I, 253) The same idea is conveyed in the *Upanishads*: "Know that Self alone that is one without a second . . . and give up all other talks."[13] (*Mundaka Upanishad*. II.ii.5). "One who thinks that He is one and he is another, does not know"[14] (*Brihadaranyaka Upanishad*, II.Iv.10). "That great, birthless, self is undecaying, immortal, undying, fearless and Brahman"[15] (*Brihadaranyaka Upanishad*, IV.iv.25).

In a letter to his brother Edward dated May 31, 1834, Emerson wrote: "Philosophy affirms that the outward world is only phenomenal and the whole concern of dimness, of tailors, of gigs, of balls, whereof man make such account is . . . an intricate dream."[16] About the *maya* of the Vedantic philosophy, he wrote: "The doctrine of the Imagination can only be rightly opened by treating it in connection with the subject of Illusions. And the Hindoos alone have treated this last with the sufficient breadth in their legend of the successive Maias of Vishnu. With them, youth, age, property, condition, events, persons, self, are only successive Maias, through which Vishnu mocks and instructs the soul." (*Journals*, IX, 302) His belief in the superiority of the Hindu thought is unmistakable, unquestionable and impeccable.

The best source that provides an insight into Emerson's thought is his famous essay "Nature," published in 1836. Here, he has formulated his philosophical and religious positions. In this essay, in the first five chapters, Emerson has reflected what Whicher calls the "Swedenborgian notion of nature as a kind of divine cryptogram, a mute gospel which man is to decipher."[17]

"Things are," Emerson wrote, "emblematic. Every appearance in nature corresponds to some state of mind." "Have mountains, and waves, and skies, no significance but what we consciously give them when we employ them as emblems of our thoughts? The world is emblematic."[18] Again he notes in one of his *Journals*: "Nature is only the foliage, the flowering, and the fruit of the soul . . . every part, therefore, exists as an emblem and sign of some fact in the soul." (IV, 282) Emerson has thus advocated" a perfect parallelism between the laws of nature and the laws of thought."[19] "Every law in nature," he wrote, "a gravity, centripetence repulsion, polarity, undulation, has a counterpart in the intellect."[20] This is the first development of Emersonian thought in *Nature's* the world is an emblem, or symbol of the spirit; it is "the memory of the mind,"[21] it is the "minor and echo" of the mind."[22] In other words, every fact in nature is a *revelation*, or as Emerson calls it *apocalypse* of the mind.[23]

The second most important development of Emerson's thought is the assertion of the primacy of ideas. The Spirit is real, the world is phenomenal; it is an effect of the Spirit. Nature depends on mind; the outside is subject to the inside. The inside alone is real; the outside is unreal, a mere manifestation, an illusion. But the impact is penetrating and impressive that it creates an impression that it is real. This is deceptive. This idea has been upheld by Emerson in his writings: "it is the uniform effect of culture on the human mind, not to shake our faith in the stability of particular phenomena as of heat, water, azote; but to lead us to regard nature as phenomenon, esteem nature as an accident and an effect."[24] "Through all its kingdoms, to the suburbs and outskirts of things, it is faithful to the cause where it had its origin. It always speaks of the Spirit. It suggests the absolute. It is a perpetual effect. It is a great shadow pointing always to the sun behind us."[25] Not only nature but arts, persons, letters, religion and objects are "subjective phenomena," or mere "shadows" of the Spirit. They are mere "fugitives." Emerson writes: "The landscape, the figures, Boston, London, are facts as fugitive as any institution past, or any whiff of mist or smoke, and so is society and so is the world. The soul looketh steadily forwards, creating as world before her, leaving world behind her. She has no dates, nor rites, nor persons, nor specialties, nor men. The soul knoweth only the soul; the web of events is the flowing robe in which she is clothed."[26]

This evidently stands for Emerson's subjective idealism, which not only asserts that the world is emblematic but it lacks reality. It is an illusion, a dream. In this respect, Emerson's thought is parallel to the Advaita theory of *Maya*. The Advaita

Vedanta propounded by Sankara says that Brahman alone is real; the world is ultimately false; the individual self is not different from Brahman (*Brahma satyam, jagan mithya, jivo Brahmaivo naparati*). "All is Brahman"[27] (*Chandogya Upanishad*, III.xiv.i). All is one, and "really there is no duality apart from the superimposition of ignorance."[28] (*Brihadaranyaka Upanishad*, IV.vi.19). In other words, *Atman* is Brahman. The world is an illusion. On account of ignorance, the individual self views what is seen as different from the real Self; and the world appears to be real as the rope is mistaken for a snake. When the ignorance is dispelled. This idea is aptly illustrated in the poem at the beginning of Emerson's essay "Illusions."

> Flow, flow the waves hated,
> Accursed, adored,
> The waves of mutation:
> No anchorage is.[29]

Towards the end of the essay Emerson not only agrees with the Vedanta doctrine of *Maya*, but even quotes from the *Vishnu Purana*:

> The early Greek philosophers Heraclitus and Xenophanes measures their force on this problem of identity. Diogenes of Apollonia said that unless the atoms were made of one stuff, they could never blend and act with another. But the Hindoos, in their sacred writings, express the liveliest feeling, both of the essential identity and of that illusion which they conceive variety to be. The notions, '*I am*' and '*This is mine*', which influence mankind are but delusions of the mother of the world. Dispel, O Lord, of all creatures, the conceit of knowledge which proceeds from ignorance. And the beatitude of man they hold to lie in being freed from fascination.[30]

Throughout the essay, Emerson uses words like "fascination," "trick," "hallucination," "deception," "disguise," to convey the idea of illusion of the changing life and the Unity which is not affected by "the waves of mutation." This idea which comes close to the Advaitic philosophy is quite clear and convincing.

Life is made of illusions. No man is free from the illusions. Emerson pointed out: "The young mortal enters the hall of the firmament . . . on the instant, and incessantly, fall snow-storms of illusions."[31] "Sleep lingers all our lifetime about our eyes, as night hovers all day in the boughs of the fir-tree."[32] "In the kingdom of illusions life is a dream, in the language of the ancients . . . we change only from bed to bed."[33] "Everything looks permanent until its secret is known. A rich estate appears to a woman a firm and lasting fact; to a merchant, one easily created out of any materials, and easily lost."[34] "All the toys that infatuate men and which they play for . . . houses, land, money, luxury, power, fame, are the self-same thing, with a new gauze or two of illusion overlaid."[35] In his essay "Montaigne," he wrote, "you believe yourselves rooted and grounded on adamant; and yet, if we uncover the last facts of our knowledge, you are spinning like bubbles, in a river, you know not whither or whence, and you are bottomed and capped and wrapped in delusions."[36]

Emerson says that these illusions have strongly affected all, irrespective of their age. He writes: "I find men victims of illusions in all parts of life. Children, youths, adults, and old men, all are led by one bauble or another."[37] "Yoganidra, the goddess of illusions . . . is stronger than the Titans, stronger than Apollo. . . . Life is a succession of lessons which must be lived to be understood. All in riddles and the key to riddle is another riddle."[38] Emerson's acceptance of *maya* as the finitising principle of Supreme Spirit is interesting and never tainted. He observed: "In fact we may come to accept it as the fixed rule and theory of our state of education, that God is a substance, and his method is illusion. The eastern sages owned the goddess Yoganidra, the great illusory energy of Vishnu, by whom an utter ignorance, the whole world is beguiled."[39] "Our eating, trading, marrying, and learning are mistaken by us for ends and realities, whilst they are properly symbols only; when we have come, by a divine leading, into the inner firmament, we are apprised of the unreality or representative character of what we esteemed final."[40] According to Emerson, actions, emotions, moods, temperament experiences are all unreal; they enter into the realm of *maya* because they hinder, in one way or another, the true perception of reality.

"There is an optical illusion," he said, "about every person we meet."[41] In his essay "Illusions," he states: "There are deceptions of the senses, deceptions of the persons and the structural, beneficent illusions of sentiment and of the intellect. There is the illusion of love, which attributes to the beloved person all which that person shares with his or her family, sex, age or condition, nay, with the human mind itself."[42] "The senses interfere everywhere and mix their own structure with all they report of."[43] These attributes supplied by the senses, Emerson says, are all wrong.

Emerson's grief over the death of his brother Charles, and on the demise of his father was exceedingly pathetic and touching. But, soon, he realized this grief was temporary and illusory. In the essay on "Experience," he reflected Hindu thought and wrote: "There are moods in which we court suffering, in the hope that here at least we shall find reality, sharp peaks and edges of truth. But it turns out to be scene-painting and counterfeit. The only thing grief has taught me is to know how shallow it is."[44] His grief, even the death of his son and father became a *maya* for him; they did not make any scar on his universal self. Never was Emerson more Vedantic than in this sense. Through *maya*, he saw his emotions, affections, and persons were useless and unreal. With the Vedantic philosophy he became a rigorous monist.

In the essay on "Experience," there are certain passages which would show how one could be an extreme illusionist. "Dream delivers as to dream, and there is no end to illusion. Life is a train of moods like a string of beads, and as we pass through them they prove to be many-coloured lenses which paint the world their own hue, and each shows only what lies in its forms."[45] The opening lines of the essay are strikingly illusory. "Where do we find ourselves? In a series of which we do not know the extremes, and believe that it has none. We wake and find ourselves on a stair; there are stairs below us, which we seem to have ascended; there are stairs above us, many a one, which go upward and out of sight. But the Genius which according to the old belief stands at the door by which we enter, and gives us the Lethe to drink, that we may tell no tales, mixed the cup too strongly, and we cannot shake off the lethargy now at noonday."[46] "Illusion, Temperament, Succession, Surface, Surprise, Reality, Subjectiveness—these are threads on the loom of time, these are the lords of life."[47] "Life itself is a hubble and scepticism, and a sleep within a sleep."[48]

For Emerson time and space are illusions. *Atman* is timeless and spaceless. In the *Katha Upanishad* (I.ii.18), it is stated: "*Atman*, we have seen, is undifferentiated, transçendental, timeless, and spaceless. It is birthless, eternal, and undecaying."[49] Time and space may look real, but they are in fact "limits." Emerson writes: "This element of illusions lends all its force to hide the values of the present time."[50] "Time is indeed the theatre and seat of illusions, nothing is so ductile and elastic. The mind stretches on hour to a century and dwarfs an age to an hour."[51] He further writes:

> The Soul circumscribes all things. As I have said, it contradicts all experience. In like manner it abolishes time and space. The influence of the senses has in most men overpowered the mind to that degree that the wall of time and space have come to look real and insurmountable; and to speak with levity of these limits is, in the world, the sign of insanity. Yet time and space are but inverse measures of the force of the soul.[52]

Emerson's doctrine of Illusion is not inconsistent with his conception of "Over-Soul" and "Self-Reliance." His "Over-Soul" is Supreme, immanent, omnipotent and transcendental. He has clearly demonstrated the non-duality of the Self, the sole reality of the Universe. But what he observed was that this Supreme Being is concealed amidst human creations, in the lower self which is false. It is the lower self that makes itself believe final, real and ultimate. It is this false knowledge, intellectual in character, which Emerson said is contradictory in a higher plane of experience, that it is relative and partial because of personal prejudices which enter so fully into the process of acquisition. This is ignorance, a false veil, which has to be broken, if Reality is to be perceived. This false veil, the *Upanishads* say, is essential for man to realize himself. Carpenter states that the illusions of reality discipline man to the understanding of the true meaning of life.[53] Gray also expressed similar opinion that Emerson exposed illusory nature of life so as to mean that God is using it for the education of the individual.[54]

The highest aim of life, Emerson says, is to realize the central Reality which lies hidden under the world of name and form. "In the history of the intellect," Emerson observes, "no more important fact than the Hindu theology, teaching that the beatitude or supreme good is to be attained through science; namely, by the perception of the real and unreal, setting aside matter, and qualities, and affections or emotions and persons, and actions, as Maias or illusions, and thus arriving at the contemplation of the one eternal Life and Cause, and a perpetual approach and assimilation to Him, thus escaping new births and transmigration."[55] The way to freedom is to realize oneself through illusions. This is Vedantic path. Emerson too has asserted it. For one who has attained the right knowledge, there is no illusion. To such a realized soul: "Nature is the true idealist when she serves us best; when, on rare days, she speaks to the imagination, we feel that the huge heaven and earth are but a web drawn around us, that the light, skies and mountains are but the painted vicissitudes of the soul."[56] Spiritual life is true and real and lasting. "The definition of *Spiritual*, says Emerson, "should be that which is its own evidence."[57] Being spiritual makes one penetrate and know the Ultimate Reality, the Over-Soul, the centre of unity, the indivisible. According to Emerson Truth is not found by self-indulgence but self-denial and self-renunciation.

Emerson's doctrine of Illusion like the Vedantic conception of *maya* is often misunderstood and misquoted. Both Sankara and Emerson agree that what appears to be unreal is not illusory and non-existent. It is the super impositions on the lower self that create misery and sorrow. It is ignorance (*avidya*), not seeing the things as they are—seeing false as false, real as real, or falsity in reality and reality in falsity—which is to be rooted out. What is required is the urgency of seeing, which will create enlightenment. For this, one need not renounce the world. It is not a renunciation of the world and kith and kin, Emerson meant, that is implied but renunciation in the spirit. To forsake the world is therefore an insult to God. Emerson says: "To be isolated is to be sick, and in so far, dead. The life of all must stream through as to make the man and the moment great."[58] Here renunciation means recognizing and realizing the presence of God in nature and the universe. "Truth the principle and Retirement and Self-denial the means of attaining." (*Journals*, X, 162-63) The same idea is conveyed in the poem "Woodnotes": "Gives all to them who all renounce."[59]

(iii) **Karma and Compensation**

The Doctrine of *karma* is an important contribution of Indian philosophy, which has often been misinterpreted and misconstrued by scholars as well as laymen. The idea of *karma* is not regarded in India as a theological doctrine or as an intellectual speculation; but it is considered to offer the only rational, logical and satisfactory explanation of all the perplexities and problems of human life. The word *karma* from the Sanskrit, literally means "action," that is, all that we do is the result of our thought. Every thought has its action and good thought reaps good action, bad thought bad action. The *Brihadaranyaka Upanishad* (III.ii.13) states: "Verily, one becomes good by good actions, bad by bad actions."[1] According to one's good and bad actions, life is happy or otherwise. As you sow, so you reap is the basic principle of the Vedic idea of *karma* (law of compensation). This law operates eternally in Nature in every turn of life. For only a mango tree will produce mangoes and a neem tree, bitter leaves. In the similar way, pure thought and kind deeds will produce unfailing happiness and their opposite will bring misery to man. This idea is exquisitely expressed in the *Upanishads.*

> According as one acts, according as one conducts himself, so does he become. The doer of good becomes good. The doer of evil be-

> comes evil. One becomes virtuous by virtuous actions, bad by bad actions.[2]
>
> As is his desire, such is his resolve; as is his resolve, such the action he performs what action (*karma)* he performs, that he procures for himself.[3] (*Brihadaranyaka Upanishad*, IV.iv.5).

On this point there is another verse in the same Upanishad which states:

> Where one's mind is attached—the inner self
> Goes thereto with action, being attached to it alone.
>
> Obtaining the end of his action,
> Whatever he does in this world,
> He comes again from that world,
> To this world of action.[4]

This is an arbitrary law; it is a true, gentle, but firm and just principle of life. When we abide by this law, our life will be endowed with richness of experience.

The law is not confined to the present life only; but its scope is extended to all the past and all the future. The law operates in both the directions. If what we are determines our future condition, then for what we are now is also determined by the past condition. Therefore, the present life is a pre-existence to that of future life. In the *Svetasvatara Upanishad* (V. 11-12), it is stated:

> According unto his deeds the embodied one successively
> Assumes forms in various conditions.
>
> Coarse and fine, many in number,
> The embodied one chooses forms according to his own qualities.
> (each) subsequent cause of his union with them is seen to be
> Because of the quality of his acts and of himself.[5]

The character which is thus determinative of one's position in the next life is formed not only by action but also by knowledge. The *Katha Upanishad* (V. 7) points out: "Either as a worm, or as a moth, or as a fish, or as a bird or as a snake, or as a tiger, or as a person, or as some other in this or that condition, he is born again here according to his deeds, according to his knowledge."[6]

In Indian philosophy the idea of *karma* is not a mere dogmatic belief or a concept; it is a fundamental law and in consonance with the modern scientific law of cause and effect. From this doctrine emerges the fact that there is no such thing as chance or fate or luck or injustice that operates the destiny of human thought and action. All the inequalities, injustice, poverty and misery which we see in the present day world are not due to any extraneous force or pre-ordination by an arbitrary Ruler, but are the inevitable results of our own mode of life and thought. Life is a field of action, and according to the seeds we sow in it do we reap. It is evident that we cannot reap what we do not sow. Sometimes, circumstances may be brightening. However overpowering and unalterable they are, they can always be overcome by good thinking and action.

Man can release from *karmic* cycle by attaining knowledge of the Self; the Ultimate reality that dwells within the inner being. The dead (*karma*) adheres not on the man who has realized himself. There are number of passages in the *Upanishads* which emphasize the efficaciousness over *karma* and rebirth of that knowledge.

The knot of the heart is loosened,
All doubts are out off,
And one's deeds (*karman*) cease

When He is seen—both the higher and the lower.[7]

(*Mundaka Upanishad*, II.ii.8).

What is soundless, touchless, formless, imperishable,
Likewise tasteless, constant, odourless,
Without beginning, without end, higher than the
Great stable—
By discerning that, one is liberated from the mouths of death.[8]

(*Katha Upanishad*, III. 15)

By knowing what is therein, Brahma-knowers
Become merged in Brahma, intent thereon,
Liberated from the womb (i.e. from rebirth).[9]

(*Svetasvatara Upanishad*, I. 7)

By knowing God there is falling off of all fetters;
With distresses destroyed, there is cessation of

Birth and death.[10] (*Svetasvatara Upanishad*, I. ii)

Emerson's doctrine of Compensation is in perfect agreement with the Vedantic doctrine of *Karma*. Vedantism had a deep influence on Emerson's thought. However highly eclectic he was, he incorporated into his personal version of transcendentalism only those parts which were most congenial to his optimistic but rather austere temperament. Consequently, he ignored the latent pessimism in the Hindu belief in the transmigration of souls and rebirth or reincarnation. His doctrine of Compensation is found defined in his essay "Compensation." The essence of this law, Emerson wrote in the essay, is that, "all things are double, one against another."[11] Emerson explained: "Every excess causes a defect; every defect an excess. Every sweet hath its sour; every evil its good."[12] While the law states that "every crime is punished," it also states that "crime and punishment grow out of one's stem. Punishment is a fruit that unsuspected ripens within the flower of the pleasure which concealed it. Cause and effect, means and ends, seed and fruit, cannot be served; for the effect already blooms in the cause, the end pre-exists in the means, the fruit in the seed."[13]

The effect we see is nothing but the fruition of a seed of action. Whether or not we may sow the seeds of thought in darkness, as the gardener unconsciously drops the seeds on the soil, the seeds must bear the fruit. It is not that an arbitrary will decrees man to be happy or unhappy. The world and human life are governed by that law and no man can escape it. As soon as man understands this law, he will be freed from the cause and effect of his actions. Emerson writes:

> Tit for tat; an eye for an eye; tooth for a tooth; blood for blood; measure for measure; love for love. Give and it shall be given you. He that watereth shall be watered himself. Thou shall be paid exactly for what thou hast done, no more, no less. Who doth not work shall not eat. Curses always recoil on the head of him who imprecates them. If you put a chain around the neck of a slave, the other end fastens itself around your own. . . . You cannot do wrong without suffering wrong.[14]

The idea of compensation also often appears in many of his other essays and poems. In his essay "Circles," he writes, "our life is an apprenticeship to the truth that around every circle another can be drawn; that there is no end in nature, but every end is a beginning; that there is always another dawn risen on mid-noon, and under every deep a lower deep opens."[15] The same idea is conveyed in his poem "Uriel." The philosophy of the reality of good and evil, which Emerson had announced in his "Divinity School Address" is presented in the first part of the poem. The parable of the archangel of the sun tells of the confusion caused among "the stern old war gods" over the circular and compensatory movement of the universe. According to this doctrine, the earth was the centre rather than the sun. The stirred devils gave their sentiment against the divine order:

> Line in nature is not found;
> Unit and universe are round;
> In vain produced, all rays return;
> Evil will bless, and ice will burn.[16]

As a youth, Emerson solely depended on traditional Christian authority for resolving the question of existence of evil in the world. He believed that man must rely on religion in order to explain the existence of evil. He queried: "if God is good, why are any of his creatures unhappy?" (*Journals*, I, 194) He did not attempt to give his own answer, but instead said: "We do not seek with vain ambition to question the abstruse and unsearchable ground of third ordination, because, it is plain matter of fact that we are incompetent to the discussion." (*Journals*, I, 195) Emerson hoped that God allows evil in the world as a counter balance necessary for the existence of good, for good can have no positive force unless there exists evil as the negative repelling force. Good and evil are two halves of one whole and like cause and effect cannot be separated. In his *Journal* of February 1822 Emerson illustrated that good and evil exist together as cause and effect. "There is a tendency in all things human to decay," he wrote, "a tendency in vice to hasten its own destruction, and in that fall, a tendency in the ruins of society towards new life."

(*Journals*, I, 87) This he did not find in the Bible, but in "Providence" which Emerson defined as "the general silent course of the Divine Government, manifested in the tendencies of human institutions and the human mind." (*Journals*, I, 86) Thus, Emerson not only expressed his inability to explain the existence of evil but also confirmed that we must simply trust in the "righteousness of the Creator."

In spite of his puritanical reliance on God, the problem of evil constantly persisted in his soul. Early in 1822, Emerson explained this conflict in a *Journal* entry on the existence of evil in the world: "No elaborate argument can remove the fact which strikes the senses, and which is the first and chief difficulty in the way of the belief of an omnipotent good principle, namely, the existence of evil in the world, and next, the great share it has in the texture of human life, and its successful opposites to virtue and happiness." (*Journals*, I, 112) Since Emerson believed in the existence of God, he had to find an explanation which would incorporate both an all-good God and the existence of evil in the world. Further, he quickly realized that simply ignoring evil's existence could not solve the problem. Emerson rejected the traditional Christian explanation of evil and a benevolent Creator because, he explained, god gave man reason so that he can examine and solve such "*mysteries*." This explanation later became his theory of compensation which he defined in 1822 as "the plan . . . whereby a succession of misfortune and suffering is counter balanced by an equal sum of happiness, and the unnatural success of vice . . . is set right again by the triumphs of virtue." (*Journals*, I, 114)

Good and evil, Emerson explained, are not the result of chance or Fortune: "the mind retires with a conviction . . . that an order is appointed, a system is proceeding." (*Journals*, II, 65) The mind, Emerson continued, "can perceive a harmonious whole, combined and over ruled by a Sublime Necessity. . . . It perceives a purpose to pain and sees how the instruction and perfection of myriads is brought about by the spectacle of guilt and punishment." (II, 65) A universe without evil may be impossible,

Emerson continued, and "happiness everywhere, as here, may be found upon the contrast of suffering." (I, 199) In April of 1823 Emerson recognized again that the ideas he had been formulating had become a "system"; this time he gave it a name "compensation." Emerson began to see these "pervading compensations" in nature's animated kingdom. "Fleetness to one animal, might to another, & cunning to a third." (II, 145-46) Also in man, "Nature mixes the Angel and the brute in the moulding of Man." (II, 146)

Emerson writes: "Every act regards itself, or in other words, integrates itself, in a two fold manner; first, in the thing, or in real nature, and secondly, in the circumstance, or in apparent nature. Men call the circumstance the retribution. The causal retribution is in the thing and is seen by the soul. The retribution in the circumstance is seen by the understanding; it is inseparable from the thing, but is often spread over a long time and so does not become distinct until after many years."[17] This law of compensation is ever present and unquestionable. Emerson was so deeply convinced of it that he observed: "Always pay; for first or last you must pay your entire debt. Persons and events may stand for a time between you and injustice, but it is only a postponement. You must pay at last your own debt."[18] This is the law that operates but we often forget it in the turmoil of our struggle and pain. We ignore the principle and see wrong and injustice apparently triumphant. If we cling to this wrong perception, we will never be released from the bondage of cause and effect. We should not do right merely because it will bring us a little satisfaction, but because it is the only way to live.

Emerson's theory of Compensation has grown over the years to become a major principle of his philosophy. During his middle years, he however became a little sceptical about its efficaciousness. His *Journals* of 1844-46 reflect the scepticism regarding his theory of compensation, often referred to during this period as a "law." He put this "law of compensation: to be the test of his own personal experiences and observations.

When Emerson was only twenty-two, he wrote in his journal that "every suffering is rewarded." (II, 72) His faith in the truth of this law is as strong as ever. "Is not the law of Compensation perfect?" he asked in his journal. In his essay "Compensation," he expressed similar optimism and faith. Emerson wrote: "The death of a dear friend, wife, brother, lover, which seemed nothing but privation, somewhat later assumes the aspect of a guide or genius."[19] But the death of his son in 1842 had terribly shaken his faith in the law. In his *Journal* of 1844, he wrote that he had "no experiences nor progress to reconcile me to the calamity whose anniversary returned the second time last Saturday . . . these ugly breaks happen there, which the continuity of theory does not compensate the astonishment of life is the absence of any appearances of reconciliation between the theory and practice of life." (*Journals*, VI, 488) Was this doctrine of Compensation, then, a false or flawed theory? Although Emerson never rejected or denied the truth of his law, he was temporarily at least sceptical of its perfection. His own personal misery makes him doubt his youthful affirmation of the truth of his law. These doubts, however, were only temporary, for his *Journals* reveal also that during his middle years Emerson's scepticism led him to stronger affirmation of his law than before. He became convinced that he, not the law, was flawed.

Emerson concluded that man was simply unable to understand all the complexities of Compensation and in 1845 he explained his optimistic belief that the future would unfold the mysteries of his law. In 1846 he revealed this optimism when he wrote in his *Journal*: "the good of *evil* will be made plain on the general scale that cannot be explained on the particular." (I, 200) From the scepticism, tension and frustration of his middle years, Emerson emerged in his late years with a confident, calm, even humorous view of life. He persisted to affirm the law's truth, he came to accept his own and man's limitations because he believed future man's power would compensate for present limitations. He found the law working in his country though it has failed the test of his personal experiences years earlier. During the Civil War, Emerson revealed in his *Journals* his strong optimism that from the evil of war would emerge the compensation good of prosperity, superior men, freedom and racial and social equality. He foresaw that the evil of war would be compensated by the good of the freedom it would make possible. "Great actions," he wrote, "have mean beginnings; poor matters point to rich ends." (*Journals*, X, 58) In 1865 his optimism in America's future greatness after the War's end was even stronger. Americans, he wrote, will eliminate, "prisons, capital punishment, slavery, tariff, disfranchisement, caste. . . . They will lead their language round the globe, & they will lead religion & freedom with them."[20]

Thus, over the years through pain and suffering, Emerson affirmed his doctrine of Compensation which worked well in his last years. He wrote: "I think it a singular and marked result that the war has established a conviction in so many minds that the right will get done; has established a chronic hope for a chronic despair." (*Journals*, X, 106) Emerson had discovered, developed and tested his law of Compensation which is in concurrence with the Vedantic doctrine of *karma*. His optimism was experience-based. The result of a lifetime marked by painful losses, failures and doubts as well as by successes, confidence and insight.

The compensation must come. Every action will bound to have a counter action. It may be positive or negative. If our labour is worthy of any recompense, the law will bring it to us. We cannot escape it. We are bound to get it. As Emerson puts it: "Human labour, through all its forms, from the sharpening of a stake to the construction of a city or an epic, is one immense illustration of the perfect compensation of the universe. The absolute balance of Give and Take, the doctrine that everything has its price—and if that price is not paid, not that thing but something else is obtained, and that it is impossible to get anything else is obtained, and that it is impossible to get anything without its price—is not less sublime in the columns of a ledger than in the budgets of states, in the laws of light and darkness, in all the action and reaction of nature."[21]

The soul that dwells within the heart is however not touched or tainted by *karmic* actions. It is free from action itself. If man realizes this, he is then freed from the chain of action and reaction. Emerson writes: "There is a deeper fact in the soul than compensation, to wit, its own nature. The soul is not compensation, but a life. The soul is. Under all this running sea of circumstance, whose waters ebb and flow with perfect balance, lies the aboriginal abyss of real being. Essence, or God, is not a relation or a part, but the whole. Being is the vast affirmative, excluding negation, self-balanced, and swallowing up all relations, parts and times within itself. Nature, truth, virtue, are the influx from thence. Vice is the absence or departure of the same."[22] "In the nature of the soul is the compensation for the irregularities of condition. The radical tragedy of nature seems to be the distinction of More or Less. How can Less not feel the pain; how not feel indignation or malevolence towards More? Look at those who have less faculty and one feels sad and knows not well what to make of it. He almost shuns their eye; he fears they will upbraid God. What should they do? It seems a great injustice. But see the facts closely and these mountainous inequalities vanish. Love reduces them as the sun melts the iceberg in the sea. The heart and soul of all men being one, this bitterness of *His* and *Mine* ceases. His is mine. I am my brother and my brother is me."[23]

These words of Emerson remind us of a beautiful passage in the *Isa Upanishad:*

> Now, he who on all being
> Looks as just (*eva*) in the Self (*Atman*).
> And on the Self as in all beings—
> He does not shrink away from Him[24] (*Isa Upanishad*, 6)
>
> In whom all beings
> Have become just (*eva*) the Self of the discerner—
> Then what delusion (*moha*), what sorrow (*soka*) is there
> Of him who perceives the unity.[25] (*Isa Upanishad*, 7)

Sorrow, hatred, jealousy, ambition, greed, lust and all such base qualities cannot touch him. He is enveloped with one spirit only, the spirit of love. When the great understanding of the light of Truth shines in our heart, all these little feelings vanish; and in their place we will find eternal joy and love unbounded. "We are idolaters of the old," Emerson again declares, "we do not believe in the riches of the soul, in its proper eternity and Omnipresence. We do not believe there is any force in today to rival or recreate that beautiful yesterday. We linger in the ruins of the old tent where once we had bread and shelter and organs, nor believe that the spirit can feed, cover and nerve us again. We cannot again find aught so dear, so sweet, so graceful. But we sit and weep in vain—the voice of the almighty saith, 'Up and onward for evermore:'"[26]

Man must rise to the heights of glory and realize the "riches of the soul." He must not grieve over his dead actions. He must march forward without brooding over what has happened or what is to happen. Past is dead and can never be revived. Future is yet to happen and therefore, it is uncertain and myth. His happiness cannot come from the past or from the future, as both are unreal and false. Similarly, he must not cling to the every changing material conditions. The real happiness derives from the present. Jiddu Krishnamurthi says, "Freedom is now, not in the future."[27] The wisest thing is therefore to live in the present. We cannot live in the present and face the reality if we lay undue stress on the past or the future. If the present is well-lived, the future will take care of itself. But we must have this wisdom of realization and we must have strength. When man realizes that he is the maker of his own life, the maker of his own bondage; that he holds the key by which he can unlock the door and enter into the realms of lasting happiness; then it gives him a new eternal happiness and peace and he will not be tempted to fall in bondage. Vedanta emphasizes this fact. A man who has attained the above state is free from the chain of action and reaction. He is not touched by the results of his own actions.

(iv) **Nityatva and Immortality**

Man is mortal. That which is born is bound to die. Birth and death are complementary and supplementary to each other; they are the two sides of the same coin. Life is changing. That which is changing is perishable and non eternal. Life thus perceived is impermanent and ever-changing. But, behind the changing and perishable is changeless and eternal. That changeless and eternal is often identified as God in various religious faiths. This God is invisible, known as Brahman, the eternal unifying principle of creation, in the *Upanishads*. Brahman alone is the Supreme Reality, changeless and eternal; the rest is all impermanent and changing. The *Brihadaranyaka Upanishad* (IV. v. 7) says: "Everything here is what this Soul is."[1] In the same *Upanishad* (IV. iv. 25) it is stated: "Verily, that great unborn Soul, undecaying, undying, immortal, fearless is Brahma."[2] The *Mundaka Upanishad* (II. Ii. 5) points out: "Him (i.e. *Brahma*) alone know as the one Soul (*Atman*). Other words dismiss."[4] The *Svetasvatara Upanishad* (I. 16) indicates: "The Soul (*Atman*) which pervades all things . . . this is Brahma"[5] The *Chandogya Upanishad* (III. X.viii.1-2) speaks: "It is the one great reality, present both in objective phenomena and in the self's activities."[6]

This single all-encompassing monistic Being is described as the one possessing as many qualities as there are in the whole of the real world which it constitutes. It is capable of all contraries:

> It moves, it moves not.
> It is far, and it is near.
> It is within all this,
> And it is outside of all this.[7] (*Isavasya Upanishad*, 4-5).

The diverse identification and constitution of this monistic Being are further expressed in the following verses:

> Being and Non-being, and what is immortal![8]
> (*Prasna Upanishad*, II.5)
> What that is, know as Being and Non-being.[9]
> (*Mundaka Upanishad*, II.ii.1)

The notion that there is much of reality which is not within the sphere of the senses, or within the world of what is called common sense experiences, expresses itself here and there in the early part of the *Upanishads*, as in the *Chandogya Upanishad* (III.xii.6).

> All beings are one-fourth of him
> Three-fourths, the immortal in the sky.[10]

Also in *Brihadaranyaka Upanishad* (I.vi.7) it is stated: "Him they see not for (as seen) he is incomplete."[11] It is by the distinction between the noumenal and the phenomenal that the apparent conflict between the One and the many is solved. In a noteworthy passage in *Brihadaranyaka Upanishad* (I.vi.3), it is declared that "Life (prana, 'breath') (a designation of the *Atman*) verily, is the Immortal. Name and form (the usual phrase signifying individuality) are the actual. By them this Life is veiled."[12] Similarly, in the same *Upanishad* (II.i.20) it is mentioned: "The mystic meaning (*Upanishad)* thereof is the 'Real of the real'."[13] The two forms of Brahma are the formed and the unformed, the mortal and the immortal, the stationary and the moving, the actual and the you. But the noumenal Brahma cannot be represented to the senses, indeed cannot be defined by any positive characteristics. "Neti, neti: Not thus! Not so!"[14] (*Ibid*., II.iii.6; III.ix.26). These two forms of Brahma are described again in *Maitri Upanishad* (VI.15): "There are, assuredly, two forms of Brahma: Time and the Timeless (*a-kala*) without parts (*a-kala*). But that which begins with the sun is Time, which has parts."[15] The thought begins to appear that it all is one, the manifold differences that seem so real in experience are not constitutive of the inner being of that One; they must be only an appearance, a phenomenon.

The Doctrine of Brahman-Atman, the Imperishable, the source of and the goal of all beings, the source of all forms of existence, the source of the activity of the senses, is well described in the following verses in the *Mundaka Upanishad*:

> That which is flaming, which is subtler than the subtle,
> On which the worlds are set, and their inhabitants—
> That is the imperishable Brahma.
> It is life *(prana*), and it is speech and mind,
> That is the real. It is immortal.[16] (*Mundaka Upanishad*, II.ii.2*)*

The man who penetrates and reaches the immortal becomes the immortal.

He who is all-knowing, all-wise,
Whose is this greatness on the earth—
He is in the divine Brahma city
And in the heaven established: The Soul (*Atman*):
Consisting of mind, leader of the life-breath and of the body,
He is established on food, controlling the heart.
By this knowledge the wise perceive
The blissful immortal that gleans forth.[17]

(*Mundaka Upanishad*, II.ii.7)

Such a soul is freed all *karma*.

The knot of the heart is loosened,
All doubts are cut off,
And one's deeds (*karman*) cease
When He is seen—both the higher and the lower.[18]

(*Mundaka Upanishad*, II.ii.8)

By meditation upon Him, by union with Him, and by
Entering into His being
More and more, there is finally cessation from
Every Illusion (*maya-nivrtti*).[19]

(*Svetasvatara Upanishad*, I. 10)

Emerson's doctrine of Immortality is based on Hindu thought. His poem "Brahma" expresses the central idea of Hindu philosophy, impersonal creative force pervading the whole universe. The same idea is conveyed in his essay "Plato" in 1850: "what is the great end of all, you shall now learn from me. It is soul—one in all bodies, pervading, uniform, perfect, preeminent over nature, exempt from birth, growth and decay. . . . The knowledge that this Spirit, which is essentially one, is in one's own, and in all other bodies, is the wisdom of one who knows the unity of things."[20] It is therefore natural and inevitable that God conceived by Emerson as above all birth and death is immortal and imperishable. Indeed, Emerson expressed this idea at the close of his essay on "Immortality," "Brahma the supreme, whoever knows him obtains whatever he wishes. The soul is not born; it does not die; it was not produced from any one. Nor was any produced from it. Unborn, eternal, it is not slain, though the body is slain, subtler than what is subtle, greater than what is great."[21]

The idea of "Brahma" was a favourite one with Emerson. He had written it in "Plato": "The conception of the fundamental unity . . . friend and foe are of one stuff; the ploughman, the plough and the furrow are of one stuff."[22] This conception he obviously derived from the Hindu thought and lay latent in his essay on the "Over-Soul," which he had written before reading any of the three Hindu books, *Vishnu Purana*, *Bhagvad Gita* and the *Katha Upanishad*. There he said: "Meantime within man is the soul of the whole; the wise silence; the universal beauty, to which every part and particle is equally related; the eternal ONE. And this deep power in which we exist and whose beatitude is all accessible to us, is not only self-sufficing and perfect in every hour, but the act of seeing and the thing seen, the seer and the spectacle, the subject and the object are one."[23] This is the theory of the Over-Soul, which is identical with the Supreme Spirit, the *adhyatman*, in the *Bhagvad Gita*, this Spirit is immanent, immortal and transcendental.

As to the question of immortality, in his youthful years, Emerson depended on the traditional views of Christianity. In the early *Journals*, he referred to life as "a journey to the throne of God" (I, 210) and "a race of preparation for the eternal struggles to reach Him." (I, 85) Of this view, he became increasingly sceptical during his middle years. He questioned the very personality of God. He doubted his existence in the human shape and form. His sceptical attitude coupled with his reading of Hindu scriptures had led him to declare that God is an impersonal creative energy, which is all-pervasive, and transcendent. From this conception Emerson inevitably confirmed that such an impersonal creative energy which is incomprehensible through an experience based on senses is immortal or everlasting. Thus, the doctrine of immortality has emerged.

Emerson's belief in the immortality of the Soul was ever strong and impeccable. He questioned himself whether there is life after death, whether life ceases with the death. The thoughts of sickness and death led him to contemplate on the "Source of Being" as he explained to his brother Edward.[24] Death always astounded him. Like any Indian mystic, Emerson deeply contemplated on the death. The problem of death worried Sankara, Buddha, Sri Ramana Maharshi, Jiddu Krishnamurthy, U.G. Krishnamurthy and scores of other mystics. These mystics had undergone death experience while living and thus had transcended it and become immortal in their life. Though Emerson had not undergone such experience, many times he found himself face to face with death and wondered if there was life eternal after earthly death. In his *Journal*, he wrote: "I said when I awoke, after some more sleepings and workings I shall lie on this mattress sick; then, dead, and through my gay entry they will carry these bones. Where shall I be then? I lifted my head and beheld the spotless orange light of the morning beaming up from the dark hills into the wide Universe." (*Journals*, IV, 335) In Hindu parlance, he had realized "the Self"—the Pure Consciousness. He had realized by direct experience that nothing existed apart from an indivisible and universal consciousness which was experienced in its unmanifest form as beingness or awareness and in its manifest form as the appearance of the universe. Sri Raman Maharshi had similar experience.[25] When he was sixteen year old school boy, alone in an upstairs room of his uncle's house in Madurai (near the southern tip of India) he was suddenly gripped by an intense fear of death. In the following minutes he went through a simulated death experience during which he became consciously aware for the first time that his real nature was imperishable and that it was unrelated to the body, the mind or the personality. From that time on his consciousness of being an individual person ceased to exist and it never functioned in him again.

Speaking of death, Emerson wrote: "The event of death is always astounding, our philosophy never reaches, never possesses it; we are always at the beginning of our catechism; always the definition is yet to be made."[26] He believed in immortality of soul. "I believe myself immortal," he wrote with firm confidence, "the beam of the balance trembles, to be sure, but settles always on the right side. For otherwise all things look so silly."[27]

The doctrine of Immortality is beautifully explained in the *Katha Upanishad* in the form of a dialogue between the Lord of death and Nachiketa, the son of Vajasravasa. At a particular ceremony Vajasravasa gave away in charities all that he had. Then, his son Nachiketa asked him: "To whom will you then give me?" The father got angry and said: "To Death." The boy then went to the house of the God of death and stayed for three nights. Recognizing him as a Brahmin guest, death told him that, since he had stayed in his house for three nights without eating, he would give him three boons, and he could choose anything. At the first boon the boy asked the Lord Yama that, when he returned to his father from the abode of death, his father should receive him without anger, tears and regret. The second boon was to explain the nature of the sacrificial fire, called also Nachiketa, which led the sacrificer to heaven. Nachiketa's third wish was most important. The boy wanted to know what happens to man after death. "Some say that he exists, but others say that he does not exist; I want to be instructed by you." (*Journals*, IV, 535) But death wanted to dissuade the boy from pressing for an answer by offering him instead all the wealth, greatness, comfort, and sovereignty over the earth. But the boy would not yield, and Death had already promised to grant whatever the boy wanted. So he had to give up and explain the nature of the *Atman* present in every man. The *Atman* is the ultimate truth, the eternal indestructible.

> The wise one [i.e. the soul] is not born, nor dies
> This one has not come from anywhere has not become anyone.
> Unborn, constant, eternal, primeval, this one
> Is not slain when the body is slain.[28] (*Katha Upanishad*, I. ii. 18)

> If the slayer think to slay,
> If the slain think himself slain
> Both these understand not,
> This one slays not, nor is slain.[29] (*Ibid.*, I.ii.9)

This *Atman* is:

> More minute than the minute, greater than the great,
> Is the Soul [*Atman*] that is set in the heart of a creature here.[30]
>
> (*Ibid.*, I.ii.20)

It is perishable, it has not birth and death. In truth there is no death for the "I," only the body is destroyed at death.

In poems like "Brahma," "Hamatreya," "Days," "Each and All," "Problem" and large parts of his essays on "Plato," "Fate," "Illusions," "Divinity School Address," "Experience," "The Over-Soul," "Spiritual Laws," "Circles" and "Compensation," Emerson revealed the intensity of his spirituality and religious attitude. In reading one gets the feeling of eternity, the impression of imperishable and eternal human values and spiritual values which we find only among the mystics or liberated souls.

In his essay on "Nature," he wrote: "There is the unspeakable but intelligible and practicable meaning of the world conveyed to man, the immortal pupil, in every object of sense. To this end of Discipline, all parts of nature conspire."[31] "We apprehend the absolute. As it were, for the first time, we *exist*. We become immortal, for we learn that time and space are relations of matter; that with a perception of truth or a virtuous will they have no affinity."[32] In a similar tone Emerson confirmed his impeccable belief in immortality of the Spirit in his essay on "History." "I believe in Eternity. I can find Greece, Asia, Italy, Spain and the Island—the genius and creative principle of each and of all eras, in my own mind."[33] "We cannot describe," he wrote, "the natural history of the soul, but we know that it is divine."[34] In his *Journals*, he recorded: "The love that is in me, the justice, the truth can never die, and that is all of me that will not die. All the rest of me is so much death,—my ignorance, my vice, my corporeal pleasure. But I am nothing else than a capacity for justice, truth, love, freedom, power. I can inhale, imbibe them for evermore. They shall be so much to me that I am nothing, they all. Then shall God be all in all. Herein is my immortality."[35]

How can we find the *Atman*, which is immortal in nature? The conditions of knowing of this great, all-pervading Soul (*Atman*) are best explained in the *Katha Upanishad*:

> This Soul [*Atman*] is not to be obtained by instruction,
> Nor by intellect, nor by such learning.
> He is to be obtained only by the one whom he chooses
> To such a one that Soul [*Atman*] reveals his own person
> [*tanim svam*][36] (I.ii.23)
>
> Not he who has not ceased from bad conduct,
> Not he who is not tranquil, not he who is not composed.
> Not he who is not of peaceful mind
> Can obtain Him by intelligence [*prajna*][37] (*Ibid.*, I.ii.24)

Mind (*manas*) is deeper than the object, reason (*buddhi*) is deeper than mind, the Logos (*mahan atman* Cosmic Reason) deeper than reason, the Unmanifest (*avyakta*) deeper than the Logos, and the Atman (*purusha*) deeper than the Unmanifest. There we find the *Atman*, deeper than which there is nothing. It is not an object towards which the senses, mind, and speech can be directed. Yet it is not Non-existence or Non-being, but Existence or Being itself.

Man becomes immortal by knowing and realizing this indwelling *Atman.* Such man is liberated from the bondage of *karma.* So, immortality holds for the highly developed mind and for the perfected individual; and not for the low mean and ignorant. Emerson writes: "Will you build magnificently for mice? Will you offer empires to such as cannot set a house or private affair in order? Here are people who cannot dispose of a day; an hour hangs heavy on their hands; and will you offer them rolling ages without end."[38] Both Sankara and Emerson consider *Atman* as timeless and spaceless. In his essay "The Over-Soul," Emerson writes: "Yet time and space are but inverse measures of the force of the soul."[39] Thus *Atman* is undifferentiated, transcendental, timeless and spaceless. It is "Birthless, eternal, and undecaying." (*Katha Upanishad*, I.ii.18)[40] Emerson shares this Advaita doctrine of release by realizing one's true identity. He expresses this idea succinctly in the essay on "Over-Soul":

> It [the Soul] calls the light its own, and feels that the grass grows and the stone falls by a law inferior to, and dependent on its nature. Behold, it saith, I am born into the great, the universal mind. I, the imperfect, adore my own perfect. I am somehow receptive of the great soul and thereby I do overlook the sun and stars and feel them to be fair accidents and effects which change and pass. More and more surges of everlasting nature enter into me, and I become public and human in my regards and actions. So come I to live in thoughts and act with energies which are immortal.[41]

When Emerson says that the sun and stars are "fair accidents" and that he is "born into the universal mind," he is in agreement with the Vedantic doctrine that the world is phenomenal and that the individual self is not different from Brahman. For Emerson the release comes from realizing this indwelling *Atman*. Thereby he becomes immortal.

The liberated man becomes one with the God in the highest scale. Emerson holds this view, when he says in his essay "Immortality" that the liberated man "is rising to greater heights, but also rising to realities; the outer relations and circumstances dying out, he entering falls and he is with God,—shares the will and the immensity of the First Cause."[42] The more and more one realizes this *Atman* in oneself, the more and more one becomes purified and universal and gets absorbed in the Absolute. In his essay on "Worship," Emerson expresses the same idea that man who is universal *now* is immortal.

> Of immortality, the soul when well employed is incurious. It is so well, that it is sure it will be well. That it is sure it will be well. It asks no questions of the Supreme Power. 'tis a higher thing to confide that if it is best we should live, we shall live,—'tis higher to have this conviction than to have the lease of indefinite centuries and millenniums and aeons. Higher than the question of our duration is the question of our deserving. Immortality will come to such as are fit for it, and he who would be a great soul in future must be great soul now. It is doctrine too great to rest on any legend, that is, on any man's experience but our own. It must be proved, if at all, from our own activity and designs, which imply in interminable future for their play.[43]

The realized man according to Emerson loses his narrow individuality which does not possess Ultimate Reality. As he becomes liberated, he is identified one with the Eternal. Such man lives in timelessness; he is immortal while being alive. Thus, *mukti* (liberation) according to the Vedanta can be achieved right now, in this life, and not in later life. Emerson also conveys the same idea. For him, the present is only a reality; and man can become truly God. He always condemned personal immortality.[44] He denied that Jesus ever preached personal immortality. In the doctrine of Immortality of the Vedanta, the "self-annihilation" means "annihilation of the lower self." The higher self is atman, which alone is real. The lower self lives in the body and enjoys the pains and pleasures of the world and unable to get over the bonds that tie it to the world, finds itself powerless and miserable. But when it realizes the higher *Atman*, he is liberated, freed from sorrow. That is, by realizing the higher *Atman*, the lower becomes great like it. But these two *Atman* are not separable at all, and exist always together. To abide in "spirit, that is without strife, death, or fear" is the substance of both the Vedanta and Emerson's teachings. It is a state of birthlessness and deathlessness—Immortality.

(v) ***Sahaja Jnana*** **and Intuition**

Emerson's conception of Over-Soul is the non-dual Reality, the true animating principle of Universe, which is identical with the Vedantic principle of Brahman. According to Emerson and the *Vedanta*, Reality is not something out there, but the ground of one's own self. It is in the inmost depth of self. Rudolf[1] observes this unifying vision as the blending of the mysticism of *Atman* in the depths of one's being. Reality both for Emerson and Sankara is valuational or axiological. The realization of it releases man from all misery and sorrow.

According to Emerson, man being at the peak of existence can realize the Universal Soul not through experience based on senses but through intuition, devoid of all experience. Emerson draws a distinction between experience and intuition, the claim that consciousness is both more inclusive and more fundamental than sensory experience. Sense experience is external, consciousness is internal, a direct self-awareness of the mind itself. Sense experience is limited, scattered, and transitory and could never of itself give man ideas of the infinite, the eternal, or the absolute. Consciousness is more fundamental than experience, since all experiences involve consciousness but not all consciousness involves experience. The mind, or self, must be aware of itself to be aware of other things. This heightened self-awareness—the mind's recognition of itself in all that it notes—is what Emerson terms intuition.

Experience is only one form of consciousness. Hence, empirically built philosophies are defective. Ideas must be traced not to the senses or experience, but to consciousness or the direct operations of the mind itself. For Emerson, Consciousness basically signifies direct awareness. Direct awareness or intuition is involved in all the operations of the mind. Indirect awareness or the representation of things by the mind is secondary and passive. Direct awareness or intuition is primary and essentially active. Emerson's Transcendentalism, therefore, asserts that the data of the senses and the whole outside world are only appearance, not ultimate reality. It is the mind's self-awareness which is a function of intuition or imagination. It envisions an infinite consciousness through its own imaginative power or intuition.

Emerson's conception of the intuitive character of the human mind and the romantically ideal nature of reality are complementary to each other. Transcendentalism drives empiricism back into the mind and finds that all truth of knowledge is intuitive; it is directly given by the operations of the mind itself. Transcendentalism admits that the only basis of truth is the self-sufficiency or self-reliance of the mind upon itself or its own flashes of awareness. Gathering evidence is secondary and derivative, immediately seeing that something is true is primary and original. Only intuition can know that mind is the only reality and that reality is infinitely rich. Emerson holds forth romantic idealism and intuition as embodiments of the quality of genius in all men. The more self-reliant men are, the more intuitive and romantically ideal they are. The whole or complete man is the intuitive or self-aware individual who romantically aspires to be without restrictions—infinite and free.

This profound realization did not come to Emerson spontaneously or in a mood of sudden inspiration, but gradually over a span of some fifty years, from the youthful observations of his adolescence to the scepticism of his middle years and, finally, to the mature and balanced view of life of his later years. In his later years, Emerson developed the major principle of his philosophy, the concept of Self-Reliance. "Self-Reliance," the essay published in 1841, is the dramatic expression of Emerson's idea of individual originality and autonomy in thought and experience.

As a youth, Emerson completely depended on Christian religion for answers to his esoteric questions, and not on insight or intuition as he developed and professed in his later years. Emerson blindly believed that man lives in God-centred Universe, that man is helpless and cannot comprehend and hence, he must totally surrender to the will of God. In his middle years, his attitude was completely changed; his attitude was one of scepticism. He questioned the authority of the Church and the Bible. He wanted to discover the truth all by himself without relying on any institution or scripture. Thus, in his middle years, all his sceptical attitude had led him to become the self-reliant "Man Thinking," and an "endless seeker," with no past at his back. (*Journals*, V, 461)

The result of this radical attitude was that Emerson had resigned the pastorate in 1842. He believed organized religion stifles an individual's freedom and thought. According to him, Calvinistic doctrines had destroyed religion of character, freedom and love. For Emerson, the "religious" man is one who listens to his own inner voice "for he alone worships." (*Journals*, VII, 44) Although he seemed to have no firm, complete and concrete answers for all philosophical questions, he was led to believe with deep conviction that only through free and independent thinking and enquiry based on the principle of Self-Reliance could man be sure of discovering the truth for himself.

For this attitudinal change, many influences had worked on Emerson in the right context during his middle years which shaped and moulded his thought and perception. The formal development of his philosophy occurred between 1825 and 1836, the period between his reading of "Lyrical Ballads" and the publication of "Nature." Emerson came under the influence of Kant even as early as 1823 when he read Dugald Stewart. His understanding of Kantian metaphysics depended in 1832 when he read F.A. Nitche's "View of Kant's Principles" which he borrowed from the Boston Athenaeum. In 1833, Emerson met Coleridge, Carlyle and Wordsworth. He read *The Critique of Pure Reason* in 1838. Kant and Coleridge were the major philosophers who influenced Emerson's thinking in the formulation of the Doctrine of Intuition. Kant's non-empirical attitude was especially a source of inspiration for Emerson. In his essay "The Transcendentalist" (1842), Emerson made his position clear by interpreting Kant's priori forms as "intuitions of the mind itself." He wrote:

> It is well known to most of my audience that the idealism of the present day acquired the name Transcendental from the use of that term by Immanuel Kant, of Koenigsburg, who replied to the sceptical philosophy of Locke, which insisted that there was nothing in the intellect which was not previously in the experience of the senses, by showing that there was a very important class of ideas or imperative forms, which did not come by experience, but through which experience was acquired; that there were intuitions of the mind itself; and he denominated them transcendental forms. The extraordinary profoundness and precision of that man's thinking was given vogue to his nomenclature, in Europe and America, to that extent that whatever belongs to the class of intuitive thought is popularly called at the present day transcendental.[2]

Though Emerson accepts Kant's notion of non-empirical elements in knowledge, he rejects Kant's limited view of intuition. He approached not only Kant but also Fichte, Schelling and other German idealists with the same critical spirit. He viewed that Coleridge was influenced by Kant. Coleridge however did not accept Kant's distinction between empirical and a priori knowledge, which is essential in Kant's philosophy. Coleridge observed that Kant erred in assuming a "higher ground" solely in the realm of morals and religion and not in all the spheres of the human nature including the speculative intellect. Furthermore, Coleridge's "intuition" is more inclusive than that of Kant. Thus, Coleridge had fallen back upon the old Greek tradition which dates back as far back as Plato and the Neo-Platonists. This tradition sees intuition not as "a process of" reasoning but as a mystic vision by which the Reality is immediately known. Emerson found in Coleridge the Greek tradition represented by Plato. Thus, the distinction between "Reason" and "Understanding" which was expounded by Coleridge in his philosophy is not original but could be attributed to Plato who distinguished between *nous* and *dianoia*. Emerson uses all these distinctions in his writings and lectures so as to bring out his own theory of Intuition more cogently and explicitly. What Emerson means by "Intuition" has parallel to the Vedantic thought of *pratyaksa jnana* (direct perception).

Reality in Vedantic sense is not an abstract metaphysical construct, but the highest Self with which the individual self is identified. The realization of this identity is *moksha*, or liberation. Brahman being immanent and manifest in the subject is not a hypothetical entity. Brahman is Being-Consciousness-Bliss (*Sat-Chit-Ananda* or *Satyam-Shivam Sundaram*). The individual self is essentially that. But Brahman cannot be realized through the modifications (*vritti*) of the mind. In the *Mundaka Upanishad* (I. i. 4), the lower (*apara*) and the higher (*para*) knowledge is distinguished. The higher is that which that Imperishable (*akshara*) is apprehended. Sankara comments that "the lower knowledge is ignorance which has to be eradicated, in as much as nothing in reality is known by knowing the objects of ignorance."[3]

Just as the *Upanishads* distinguish between lower knowledge and higher knowledge, Emerson also distinguishes between Understanding and Reason. Emerson's concept of Reason is virtually the same as the higher knowledge of the *Upanishads*. Of this Reason, Emerson writes: "Reason is the highest faculty of the soul—what we mean often by the soul itself; it never *reasons*, never proves, it simply perceives; it is vision. The Understanding toils all the time, compares, contrives, adds, argues, nearsighted, dwelling in the present, the expedient, the customary. Beasts have some understanding but to Reason. Reason is potentially in every man—Understanding in every man in different degrees of strength. The thoughts of youth and first thoughts are the revelations of Reason."[4] For Emerson Reason is not a faculty but the soul itself. It is potentially perfect in all people. Reason is the Self, the Being, and the vision and Being become identical.

In the same way, in the *Upanishads* it is stated that Reality is vision or consciousness, that the sole reality is the Self, that the idea of non-self is imposed upon Self by ignorance, and that knowledge removes this false notion. "He who meditates upon each of this totality of aspects does not know, for it is incomplete. . . . The Self alone is to be meditated upon for all these are unified in It"[5] (*Brihadaranyaka Upanishad*, I.iv.7). The *Chandogya Upanishad* (VII.xv.2) mentions, "There is nothing apart from the Infinite; the Infinite is all."[6] The *Mundaka Upanishad* (II.ii.11) quotes: "The world is nothing but Brahman, the highest."[7] The (*Brihadaranyaka Upanishad*, II.v.9) states: "This self, the perceiver of everything is Brahman"[8] Right knowledge dispels the idea of not being Brahman and not being all. Emerson writes: "Our compound nature differentiates us from God, but our Reason is not to be distinguished from the divine essence." (*Journals*, III, 235) "Its [Reason's] attributes are Eternity and Intuition. We belong to it, not it to us. Human individuality is an upstart just now added to this Eternal Beatitude."[9] Reason is, therefore, the same as the Universal Soul. Reason is not mine or thine or his but we are Its. Understanding, on the contrary, is smoke, an accident; it works as if it were real.

Emerson observes that if this higher knowledge is to be known, man must be self-reliant. Man must rely on himself. In his *Journals* of 1844-46, Emerson observed that if man wants to achieve this self-reliance which is paramount in comprehending the abstruse truths, he must reject all beliefs and traditions which are not his own; he must disband all authority; he must allow himself solitude and only selective society; and he must live in the present and not look to the past for answers, not spend his time hoping for the future.

Emerson recognized the importance of solitude in order to achieve self-reliance. "To go into solitude," his essay on "Nature" begins, "a man needs to retire as much from his chamber as from society."[10] In the *Bhagvad Gita* it is stated that the seeker after Brahman should remain in seclusion, alone with the mind, and body controlled, free from desire, and having no possessions. Thus, keeping the mind balanced, the *Yogin* attains peace and happiness. Emerson declares in almost the same terms as the *Bhagvad Gita* that retirement from society to a solitary place leads him to tranquillity and serenity. He writes:

> Crossing a bare common in snow puddles, at twilight, under a clouded sky, without having in my thoughts any occurrence of special good fortune, I have enjoyed perfect exhilaration, I am glad to the brink of fear. In the woods, too, a man casts off his years, as the snake his slough, and at what period so ever of life is always a child. In the woods is perpetual youth. Within these plantations of God, a decorum and sanctity reign, a perennial festival is dressed, and the guest sees not how he should tire of them in a thousand years. In the woods, we return to reason and faith. There I feel that nothing can befall me in life,—no disgrace, no calamity leaving me my eyes, which nature cannot repair.[11]

Emerson observed that even the family could interfere with the development of self-reliance. This sounds somewhat cold and bitter. Critics have often testified it as his lack of social ease and inability to express his affection and love. But Emerson rejected such personal love in favour of the Universal and impersonal love of genius. "Understanding me when I say, I love you, it is your genius and not you." (*Journals*, IX, 377) "I like man, but not men." (*Journals*, VII, 165) But at the same time, he did not reject society. He observed that man must live within the society, as it is essential requirement to develop his genius and achieve inward solitude amidst all. Man must achieve a balance between society and solitude. Emerson explained in his essay "Self-Reliance": "It is easy in the world to live after the world's opinions; it is easy in solitude to live after our own; but the great man is he who in the midst of a crowd keeps with perfect sweetness the independence of solitude." (*Journals*, VII, 48) Emerson did not advocate that man should become hermit in caves. He observed that total solitude is just as unprofitable and undesirable as total immersion in society. The way, he concluded, was balance. According to him, man must take the best which society has to offer—its culture—and use it to stimulate his own inner growth.

Emerson also opposed philanthropy and charity which do not help increase the giver's self-reliance. "It is easy to live for others; everybody does," he wrote in 1845, "I call on you to live for yourselves." (*Journals*, VII, 32-33) He also opposed community living such as advocated at Brook Farm and at Fruit Lands, two Utopian communities by his friends and acquaintances. Such community life went against the spirit of Emerson's self-reliance and individualism. The communities, according to him, would develop only physical self-reliance but not the real self- or soul-reliance. He explained his position in his 1845 *Journal*: "No, it is not the part of merit of a man to make him stone with his own hands, or cook and bake his own dinner; another can do it better and cheaper; but it is his essential virtue to carry out into action, his own dearest ones, to dare to do what he believes and loves." (VII, 78) Therefore, man must now and then, withdraw from unnecessary society if he wants to be truly self-reliant, "for the secret of God will not impart himself to us for tea-table talk."[12]

Emerson also insists that man must live in the present seeking neither answers from the past nor comfort and hope from the future. In his essay, "Self-Reliance," Emerson called on men to reject the past ("Live ever in a new day") as well as the future ("There is somewhat low even in hope").[13] A man, Emerson added, cannot become self-reliant until he lives "in the present, above time." (*Journals*, VI, 523) According to him, the ideas and thoughts of past man, like the society of present man, can interfere with a man's development of self-reliance. The truly self-reliant man, Emerson wrote in his *Journal*, "buries in oblivion the crowded historical past, sink religions, philosophies, nations, persons, to legends . . . and makes the thought of the moment the key to the universe and egg of history to come." (VII, 159)

He focused on the life itself, not on a future after life. Life to the young Emerson was merely a journey to the next life. But the mature Emerson recognized the value of the present life. "When I speak of miracles," he wrote in his *Journal*, "I am never thinking of dead man." (VII, 441) By living in the future a man would miss all earning offered by the present "prophecy," he wrote in 1846, "is not more sacred than is knowledge of the present." (*Journals*, VII, 160) So, Emerson advised man to concentrate on the present, on "the riches that surround him." This is essential, Emerson strongly believed, to the achievement of self-reliance.

While developing this genius, man should not become extremely self-centred. Man is important, he said, he is not all. Man's power and even his potential might be limited if he becomes self-centred. In his essay, "The Transcendentalist," Emerson has been deeply convinced of the unlimited power of the self-reliant man to will great thoughts; he believed in the "perpetual openness of the human mind to new influx of light and power."[14] At the same time, Emerson did not dismiss the limitations of man. Man is limited and not divine in its truest sense. He cannot create his own universe; he cannot will the knowledge to explain the mysteries of the universe and of his own existence. Man is, therefore, not all but only part of a larger scheme: "Man is only a piece of the universe made alive." (*Journals*, VII, 104) So, it may be seen that though Emerson in his middle years strongly affirmed self-reliance, he was somewhat disillusioned. He also had come to believe that total self-reliance is impossible.

He came to accept the limitations. But, these limitations are temporary and not everlasting. Surely and certainly, as Emerson believed that man could really overcome these limitations. Thus, his disturbing reality of what man is would be balanced by his strong optimism in what man will be.

In his late years (1844-46) Emerson came to believe that man unlike other creatures is fundamentally evolving. This natural evolution insures man would be free from the limitations. He had come to assert confidently that a natural tendency exists in man and in nature toward the better. The fact of present limitations which Emerson viewed in his middle years was balanced by his profound and amazing faith in future power, calm acceptance and confident optimism which marked his later years. He still believed that man achieves self-reliance only by rejecting traditions, others' beliefs, by disowning the past, by achieving a balance between society and solitude, and by living in the present, not looking into the future. He expressed a strong optimism and confidence in the powers of future man. "Things once not possible are probable now." (*Journals*, X, 194) His confidence in the power of future man was strong; the man of the future, he believed, will control his own universe, and will "deal with the old ball of the Earth as a carpenter does with wood."[15] He advised man to trust his own deep insight, the best source of comprehending the truth, for future guidance and answers. He said: "Nothing of religious tradition, not the immortality of the soul is credible after we have experienced an insight, a thought."[16]

Emerson noted that each man must discover this wisdom for himself; each generation must discover for itself. He who achieves this self-reliance becomes the ideal, contributing immense to the cause of peace and progress of humanity. In his essay "Self-Reliance," he described that "great man . . . who in the midst of a crowd keeps with perfect sweetness, the independence of solitude."[17] This maintaining "perfect sweetness" and "the independence of solitude" by each individual will make human life noble, dignified, enriching and beautiful.

NOTES

1. Hyatt H. Waggoner, *Emerson as Poet* (Princeton University Press, 1974), p. 16.
2. *Ibid.*
3. George Santayana, "Emerson," *Interpretations of Poetry and Religion* (New York, 1900), pp. 217-33.
4. Robert Frost, "On Emerson," *Dae Oalcus* (Fall 1959), pp. 712-19.
5. *Emerson and Asia*, p. 104.
6. Bliss Perry, *Emerson Today* (Princeton University Press, 1931), p. 59.
7. *Indian Philosophy* (London, George Allen & Unwin, 1966), I, p. 63.
8. S.N. Dasgupta, *A History of Indian Philosophy* (Cambridge, 1951), I, p. 10.
9. P. Nagaraja Rao, *Introduction to Vedanta* (New Delhi, 1958) Chapter IV, pp. 43-49.
10. Pramahamsa Yogananda, *Autobiography of a Yogi* (Rider and Company, London, 1952), p. 71.
11. *Ibid.*
12. *Indian Philosophy*, I, p. 128.
13. Max Muller supposed the date to be 1200 B.C.: Hang 2400 B.C.; Tilak, 4000 B.C.; S.N. Dasgupta, *A History of Indian Philosophy*, Vol. I, p. 10. See also Macdonell, *Sanskrit Literature*, p. 8; Monier Williams, *Indian Wisdom*, p. 5.
14. *A Critical Survey of Indian Philosophy*, p. 17.
15. The different schools of philosophical systems and their founders with their important *Sutras* (aphorisms) are: Gautama, the founder of the Nyaya School, composed his *Nyaya Sutras*; Kanada, the founder of the Vaisesika School, *The Vaisesika Sutras*; Jaimini, the founder of the Mimamsa School, the *Mimamsa Sutras*; Badarayana, the founder of the Vedanta school, the *Vedanta Sutras*, also called *Brahma Sutras*; Patanjali, the founder of the *Yoga School*, the *Yoga Sutras*; Charvaka whose name is also given as Brhaspati, the founder of the Charvaka School, the *Brhaspati Sutras*; Kapila, the founder of the Sankhya School, the *Sankhya Sutras*.
16. Qtd. Paramhamsa Yogananda, *Autobiography of a Yogi*, p. 71.
17. V.M. Apte, trans., *Brahma-Sutra Sankara Bhasya: Brahma Sutras with Sankara's Commentary* (Bombay, 1960), p. 61.

18. Swami Mahavananda, trans., *The Brihadaranyaka Upanishad with the Commentary of Sankaracharya* (Calcutta: Advaita Ashrama, 1975), p. 517.
19. *Ibid.*, p. 469.
20. *Complete Works*, Vol. I, p. 63.
21. *Works*, Vol. II, p. 70.
22. *Ibid.*, p. 268.
23. *Ibid.*, p. 271. "Over-Soul."
24. *Works*, Vol. I, p. 271.
25. *Works*, Vol. II, pp. 269-70. "Over-Soul."
26. *Works*, Vol. III, p. 69. "Experience."
27. G.E. Woodberry, *Emerson* (New York, 1907), pp. 153-54.
28. *Works*, Vol. X, p. 534. See also G.E. Woodberry, Emerson, p. 56.
29. F.I. Carpenter, *Ralph Waldo Emerson*, xxviii.
30. See *Mass. Quarterly Review*, III, pp.117-18.
31. O.B. Frothingham, *The Religion of Humanity*, p. 39.
32. *Transcendentalism in New England: A History* (New York, 1908), p. 227.
33. Robert Ernest Hume, trans., *The Thirteen Principal Upanishads* (Delhi: Oxford University Press, 1983), pp. 57 & 353.
34. *Ibid.*, p. 144.
35. *Ibid.*, p. 372.
36. *Ibid.*, p. 397.
37. *Ibid.*, p. 118.
38. *The Selected Writings of Ralph Waldo Emerson*, p. 809.
39. Swami Paramananda, *Srimad Bhagvad Gita* (Boston, 1913), pp. 13-14.
40. *Works*, Vol. VI, p. 49.
41. *The Selected Writings of Ralph Waldo Emerson*, p. 809.
42. F.O. Matthiesen, *The Oxford Book of American Verse* (Oxford University Press, New York, 1968), p. 70.
43. *Works*, Vol. I, p. 12, "Nature."
44. *Ibid.*
45. *The Oxford Book of American Verse*, p. 71.
46. *Ibid.*, pp. 44-45.
47. *Works*, Vol. I, p. 58. "Nature."
48. *Ibid.*, p. 61. See also p. 64.
49. *Ibid.*, pp. 41-42. "Nature."
50. *Ibid.*, p. 48.
51. *Ibid.*, p. 44.

52. *Ibid.*, p. 62.
53. *Ibid.*, p. 48.
54. *Works*, Vol. I, p. 64. "Nature."
55. *Works*, Vol. IV, p. 49. "Nature."
56. *The Thirteen Principal Upanishads*, p. 366.
57. *Ibid.*, p. 367.
58. *Ibid.*
59. *Works*, Vol. I, pp. 73-74. "Nature."
60. *The Thirteen Principal Upanishads*, p. 343.
61. *Works*, Vol. XII, p. 8.
62. *Works*, Vol. II, p. 124.
63. *Works*, Vol. II, p. 292. "The Over-Soul."
64. *The Thirteen Principal Upanishads*, p. 363.
65. *Ibid.*
66. *Ibid.*, p. 81.
67. *Ibid.*
68. *Ibid.*, p. 287.
69. Swami Prabhavananda and Christopher Isherwood, trans. *Shankaracharya's Crest-Jewel of Discrimination* (California: Vedanta Press, 1947), pp. 66-67.
70. *Works*, Vol. I, p. 120.
71. *Works*, Vol. II, p. 11. "History."
72. Ralph L. Rusk, ed. *The Letters of Ralph Waldo Emerson*, Vol. I, p. 409.
73. *Works*, p. 127. "Divinity School of Address."
74. *Works*, Vol. I, p. 375.
75. *Works*, Vol. XII, p. 62.
76. *Works*, Vol. IV, p. 186. "Montaigne."
77. *The Code of Manu*, VI, p. 160 (Monier Williams, trans.).
78. *Works*, Vol. XI, p. 236.
79. *Works*, Vol. VI, p. 6.
80. *Ibid.*, X, p. 36. See also, p. 63; III, pp. 125, 126.
81. *Works*, Vol. IV, p. 98. "Swedenborg."
82. *Ibid.*, p. 80.
83. *Ibid.*, p. 103.
84. *Ibid.*, p. 23.
85. *Ibid.*, Vol. IV, p. 56. "Plato."
86. *Ibid.*, p. 271.
87. *Ibid.*, p. 57. "Plato."
88. *Ibid.*, p. 18. "Uses of Great Men."

89. *Ibid.*, p. 55. "Plato."
90. *Ibid.*, pp. 253-55.
91. *Ibid.*, p. 28. "Uses of Great Men."
92. *Ibid.*, Vol. II, p. 296. "The Over-Soul."
93. *Works*, Vol. IV, p. 534.
94. Pratap Chunder Mazoomdar, *Emerson as Seen from India*, p. 102.
95. Heramba Chandra Maitra, "Emerson from an Indian Point of View," *Harvard Theological Review*, Vol. IV, p. 417.

(ii) **Maya and Illusion**

1. F.I. Carpenter, *Emerson and Asia*, pp. 39-66; John S. Harrison, *The Teachers of Emerson* (New York: Haskell House, 1966), pp. 3-31; Lenneth Walter Cameron, *Emerson the Essayist* (Hartford: Transcendental Books, 1945).
2. *The Thirteen Principal Upanishads*, p. 208.
3. *Ibid.*, p. 143.
4. *Ibid.*, p. 262.
5. *Ibid.*, p. 425.
6. *Ibid.*, p. 92.
7. *Ibid.*, p. 104.
8. *Ibid.*, p. 404.
9. *Ibid.*, p. 232.
10. *Ibid.*, p. 348.
11. Shankara's Commentary on *Chandogya Upanishad*, V.x.2; Jha, p. 254.
12. *The Thirteen Principal Upanishads*, p. 83.
13. *Ibid.*, p. 372.
14. *Ibid.*, p. 100.
15. *Ibid.*, p. 144.
16. Ralph L. Rusk, ed., *Letters*, I, p. 412; also see *Journals*, Vol. III, pp. 35, 481.
17. Whicher, *Freedom and Fate*, p. 53.
18. *Works*, Vol. I, p. 32.
19. *Works*, Vol. VIII, p. 53.
20. *Ibid.*, Vol. III, p. 211.
21. *Ibid.*, Vol. I, p. 188.
22. *Ibid.*, Vol. X, p. 185.
23. *Ibid.*, Vol. I, p. 53.
24. *Ibid.*, p. 149.
25. *Ibid.*, Vol. VIII, p. 223.

26. *Ibid.*, Vol. II, p. 274.
27. *The Thirteen Principal Upanishads*, p. 209.
28. *Ibid.*, p. 147.
29. *Ibid.*, Vol. VI, p. 307.
30. *Ibid.*, p. 324.
31. *Ibid.*, Vol. VI, p. 325. "Illusions."
32. *Ibid.*, Vol. III, p. 45.
33. *Journals*, Vol. VIII, pp. 414-15. See also *Works*, Vol. VI, p. 222.
34. *Works*, Vol. II, p. 303. "Circles."
35. *Ibid.*, Vol. VI, p. 40. See also *Journals*, Vol. IX, p. 322.
36. *Ibid.*, Vol. IV, p. 155, "Montaigne."
37. *Ibid.*, Vol. VI, p. 313.
38. *Ibid.*
39. *Ibid.*, Vol. IV, p. 178. See also *Journals*, Vol. VIII and Vol. X, pp. 157-60.
40. *Ibid.*, Vol. XII, p. 19. See also Vol. III, p. 306.
41. *Ibid.*, Vol. III, pp. 51-52. "Experience."
42. *Ibid.*, Vol. VI, p. 319. "Illusions". See also *Works*, Vol. II, p. 222.
43. *Ibid.*, Vol. III, p. 311. "Illusions."
44. *Ibid.*, Vol. III, pp. 48-49. "Experience."
45. *Ibid.*, p. 50.
46. *Ibid.*, p. 45.
47. *Ibid.*, pp. 82-83.
48. *Ibid*, p. 65.
49. *The Thirteen Principal Upanishads*, p. 349.
50. *Works*, Vol. VII, p. 173.
51. *Ibid.*, Vol. VII, p. 317. "Old Age". See also Vol. VI, p. 319.
52. *Ibid.*, Vol. II, p. 27.
53. *Emerson and Asia*, pp. 130, 131.
54. H.D. Gray, *Emerson: A Statement of New England Transcendentalism as Expressed in the Philosophy of its Chief Exponent* (California: Stanford University), p. 42.
55. *Journals*, Vol. X, p. 162. See also *Works*, Vol. III, pp. 59-60.
56. *Works*, Vol. VIII, p. 26. "Imagination."
57. *Ibid.*, Vol. III, p. 53. "Experience."
58. *Ibid.*, Vol. XII, p. 21. "Powers and Laws of Thought."
59. *Ibid.*, Vol. IX, p. 57.

(iii) **Karma and Compensation**

1. *The Thirteen Principal Upanishads*, p. 110.

2. *Ibid.*, p. 140.
3. *Ibid.*
4. *Ibid.*, p. 141.
5. *Ibid.*, p. 407.
6. *Ibid.*, p. 357.
7. *Ibid.*, p. 373.
8. *Ibid.*, p. 353.
9. *Ibid.*, p. 395.
10. *Ibid.*, p. 397.
11. Brooks Atkinson, ed. *The Selected Writings of Ralph Waldo Emerson* (New York, 1950), p. 179.
12. *Ibid.*, p. 173.
13. *Ibid.*, p. 176.
14. *Ibid.*, p. 179.
15. *Ibid.*, p. 279.
16. *Ibid.*, p. 764.
17. *Ibid.*, p. 176.
18. *Ibid.*, p. 281.
19. *Ibid.*, p. 188.
20. *Selected Writings*, ed. Gilman, p. 176.
21. *The Selected Writings of Ralph Waldo Emerson*, p. 182.
22. *Ibid.*, p. 185.
23. *Ibid.*, p. 187.
24. *The Thirteen Principal Upanishads*, p. 363.
25. *Ibid.*
26. *The Selected Writings of Ralph Waldo Emerson*, p. 188.
27. J. Krishnamurti, *The Awakening of Intelligence* (New York: Avon, 1976), p. 113.

(iv) *Nityatva* and Immortality

1. *The Thirteen Principal Upanishads*, p. 146.
2. *Ibid.*, p. 144.
3. *Ibid.*, p. 301.
4. *Ibid.*, p. 372.
5. *Ibid.*, p. 397.
6. *Ibid.*, p. 212.
7. *Ibid.*, p. 363.
8. *Ibid.*, p. 381.
9. *Ibid.*, p. 372.
10. *Ibid.*, p. 209.

11. *Ibid.*, p. 82.
12. *Ibid.*, p. 92.
13. *Ibid.*, p. 95.
14. *Ibid.*, pp. 97 & 125.
15. *Ibid.*, p. 434.
16. *Ibid.*, p. 372.
17. *Ibid.*, p. 373.
18. *Ibid.*
19. *Ibid.*, p. 396.
20. *Works*, Vol. IV, pp. 49-50.
21. Qtd. F.I. Carpenter, *Emerson and Asia*, pp. 119-20.
22. *The Selected Writings of Ralph Waldo Emerson*, p. 478.
23. *Ibid.*, p. 262.
24. Ralph L. Rusk, ed. *The Letters of Ralph Waldo Emerson*, I, p. 315.
25. David Godman, ed., *Be As You are: The Teachings of Ramana Maharshi* (New Delhi: Penguin, 1985), pp. 1-4.
26. Also See T.M.P. Mahadevan, *Ramana Maharshi: The Sage of Arunachala* (A Mandala Book, London: Unwin Paperbacks, 1977), p. 12.
27. He then lay down stretching his limbs out and holding them stiff as though *rigor mortis* had set in. He held his breath and kept his lips tight, closed, so that till outward appearance his body resembled a corpse, "Well, this body is now dead. It will be carried to the funeral pyre and there reduced to ashes. But do I die with the death of this body? Is the body I? it is silent and inert; but I feel the full force of any personality and even the voice of the 'I' within me, apart from it. So I am the Spirit transcending the body by death. That means that I am the deathless Spirit." The realization came to him in a flash. He perceived the truth directly. 'I' was something very real, the only real thing. Fear of death had vanished once and for all.
28. *The Thirteen Principal Upanishads*, p. 344.
29. *Ibid.*, p. 342.
30. *Ibid.*, p. 344.
31. *The Selected Writings of Ralph Waldo Emerson*, p. 26.
32. *Ibid.*, p. 32.
33. *Works*, Vol. II, p. 9. "History."
34. *Works*, Vol. I, p. 223. "The Method of Nature."
35. *Journals*, Vol. IV, pp. 127-28; Vol. X, p. 278.
36. *The Thirteen Principal Upanishads*, p. 345.

37. *Ibid.*
38. *Works*, Vol. VIII, p. 348. "Immortality."
39. *Works*, Vol. II, p. 272. "The Over-Soul."
40. *The Thirteen Principal Upanishads*, p. 349.
41. *Works*, Vol. II, p. 196. "The Over-Soul."
42. *Works*, Vol. VIII, p. 349. "Immortality."
43. *Works*, Vol. VI, pp. 238-39, "Worship." Also See *Journals*, Vol. VII, p. 408.
44. *Works*, Vol. VIII, p. 348.

(v) *Sahaja Jnana* and Intuition

1. Rudolf Otto, *Mysticism of East and West* (New York: Macmillan, 1972), Chapter 4.
2. *Works*, Vol. I, pp. 339-40. "The Transcendentalist."
3. *Gambhirananda*, II, p. 86. *The Thirteen Principal Upanishads*, p 366.
4. *The Letters of Ralph Waldo Emerson*, I, pp. 412-13. Qtd. Cameron, *Emerson the Essayist*, I, pp. 184-85.
5. *The Thirteen Principal Upanishads*, p. 82.
6. *Ibid.*, p. 258.
7. *Ibid.*, p. 373.
8. *Ibid.*, p. 103.
9. Qtd. Cameron, *Emerson the Essayist*, I, p. 192.
10. *Works*, Vol. I, p. 7. "Nature."
11. *Ibid.*, pp. 9-10.
12. *The Selected Writings of Ralph Waldo Emerson*, pp. 152-53.
13. *Ibid.*, p. 157.
14. *Ibid.*, p. 50.
15. *Selected Writings*, ed. Gilman, p. 179. See also Journals, Vol. X, p. 194.
16. *Ibid.*, p. 175; *Journals*, Vol. X, p. 11.
17. *The Selected Writings of Ralph Waldo Emerson*, p. 150.

Chapter IV

Idealism and Spirituality

Emerson's romantic idealism, his mystical aspirations and metaphysical quest, his philosophic Utopianism, his moral optimism, when taken together make him a great spiritual leader of his times. His was a unified vision, embodied in Vedantic mysticism. Emerson's spirituality was determined by his idealism and mysticism. He was a spiritual revolutionary who rejected all dogmas including the dogma of Christianity and stubbornly refused to accept any other external voice except the voice of the inner heart. He purely relied on the inner soul for understanding the greater truths of the nature of the universe, the nature of the Ultimate Reality, the place of man in the universe and man's duty.

Emerson's philosophy was a curious mixture of the idealistic and mystical traditions of the Vedantic thought and philosophy. His philosophy comprising doctrines and ideas like Over-Soul, self-reliance, divinity of human nature, freedom of inquiry, spiritual emancipation, religious freedom, freedom of expression, self-sufficiency of the individual is in perfect agreement with the philosophy illustrated in the *Upanishads*. The influence of Hindu philosophy on Emerson is unquestionable and ever strong. The purpose of the chapter is to study Emerson's idealism and spirituality in the context of Vedantic idealism and spirituality.

Idealism is fundamental to Emerson's thought. His idealism is shaped to a great extent by the idealism of Vedanta. The view that there is a single unifying energy principle, which is impersonal in character, omnipotent, omniscient, omnipresent, eternal and transcendental, operating the whole infinite universe can be realized here, now, in this life, not through sense organs, but through intuition, is very much identical with the Vedantic concept of Brahman, the impersonal God. The realization of this leads to liberation. This monistic idealism is central not only to Emerson's thought but also to the Transcendentalists as a whole. Emerson acknowledges, in unequivocal terms, his love for the Indian religion: "The Indian teaching, through its clouds of legends, has yet a simple and grand religion, like a queenly countenance seen through a rich veil. It teaches to speak the truth, love others as yourself, and to despise trifles. The East is grand, and makes Europe a land of trifles."[1]

Transcendentalism is an idealistic philosophy and it is only as an idealist that Emerson comes very close to the Upanishadic philosophy. The best source that provides an insight into Emerson's thought is his essay on "Nature" which epitomizes his philosophical and religious positions. In the first five sections, Emerson demonstrates how nature is an emblem of the spirit. These five sections of "Nature" reflect what which calls the "Swedenborgian notion of nature as a kind of divine cryptogram, a mute gospel which man is to decipher."[2] In the last three sections, Emerson moves from idealism to spirituality. "Things are," Emerson writes, "emblematic. Every appearance in nature corresponds to some state of mind." "Have mountains, and waves, and skies, not significance but what we consciously give them when we employ them as emblems of our thoughts? The world is emblematic."[3] Emerson records in his journals that nature "is only the foliage, the flowering, and the fruit of the soul . . . every part therefore exists as an emblem and sign of some fact in the soul."[4] Emerson is thus advocating a "perfect parallelism between the laws of thoughts."[5] "Every law in nature," he writes, "as gravity, centripetence, repulsion, polarity, undulation, has a counterpart in the intellect."[6] This is the first movement of thought of Emerson we find in "Nature": "The world is an emblem, or symbol of the spirit; it is 'the memory of the mind'."[7] In other words, every fact in nature and even the most material of sensations can be seen as *revelation*. Or, as Emerson calls it *apocalypse* of the mind.[8]

From the apocalypse of the mind, Emerson moves to assert that the Spirit is real and the world is phenomenal; it is an effect of the spirit. Idealism implies that the phenomenal world is not the ultimate reality. It has not *paramarthick satta.* In the essay he writes: "It is the uniform effect of culture on the human mind, not to shake our faith in the stability of particular phenomena as of heat, water, azote; but to lead us to regard nature as phenomenon, not substance; to attribute necessary existence to spirit; to esteem nature as an accident and an effect."[9] In other words, the basic assumption of idealism is that the ideas are real and the objective world is unreal. Moreover, idealism emphasizes that mind is prior to matter and not the product of matter. Emerson fully subscribes to this view: "Mind is the only reality, of which men and all other natures are better or worse reflectors."[10] "Through all its kingdoms to the suburbs and outskirts of things, it is faithful to the cause whence it had its origin. It always speaks of the Spirit. It suggests the absolute. It is a perpetual effect. It is a great shadow pointing always to the sun behind us."[11]

In "Nature," Emerson writes in a similar vein and admits that true reality lies behind the temporal phenomenon. He mentions Vyasa and Berkeley as the greatest idealist thinkers. "The first and last lesson of religion is, 'the things that are seen, are temporal; the things that are unseen, are eternal.' It puts an affront upon nature. It does that for the unschooled, which philosophy does for Berkeley and Vyasa."[12] Not only are nature, art, persons, letters, religion and objects "subjective phenomenon" and "shadows" which the spirit casts, they are also "fugitive." Emerson writes:

> Things we now esteem fixed shall, one by one, detach themselves like ripe fruit from our experience, and Fall. The landscape, the figures, Boston, London are facts as fugitive as any institution past, or any whiff of mist or smoke, and so is society and so is the world. The soul looketh steadily forwards, creating a world before her, leaving worlds behind her. She has no dates, nor rites, nor persons, nor specialties, nor men. The soul knoweth only the soul; the web of events is the flowing robe in which she is clothed.[13]

Emerson has revealed himself through the first part of "Nature" as an idealistic. In the idealistic philosophy, ultimate truth is an essence, a pure consciousness, not matter. Behind and within the phenomena there is a spiritual absolute; and the multitude of things and events are manifestations of that Ultimate Reality. This Reality is called Brahman in Hinduism and the ultimate principle, the Over-Soul, the World-Soul or the ground of Being by Emerson and other idealists. Emerson's thought is parallel to the Advaita theory of *Maya*. According to the Advaitic philosophy as advocated by Sankara, Reality is One; all is One; the world of name and form is not real; it is only an appearance. In *Chandogya Upanishad* (II.i.4) it is stated: 'All product . . . is mere name . . . the sense is that there is no real entity in the shape of the product; it exists in name only being based upon words."[14] "All is Brahman; diversity is only an appearance due to ignorance that all is essentially one."[15] (*Chandogya Upanishad*, III.xiv.1)

The "Ultimate principle" is indefinable and ungraspable in nature, and is one. In Transcendental idealistic philosophy, dualism is not tenable, and one cannot accept philosophically the existence of two independent absolutes. The same idea is embedded in the *Upanishads* that Brahman is the only principle that is the inner essence of all things. It is infinite in nature and beyond all concepts, ideas, doctrines, dogmas, isms and so on. The *Mundaka Upanishad* (I.i.7) describes: "As a spider emits and draws in [its thread]. As herbs arise on the earth, As the hairs of the head and body from a living person, So from the Imperishable arises everything here."[16] Emerson expresses these ideas in "Nature": "Idealism sees the world in God. It beholds the whole circle of persons and things, of actions and events, of country and religion, not as painfully accumulated, atom after atom, act after act, in an aged creeping past, but as one vast picture which God points on the instant eternity for the contemplation of the soul."[17] Christianity does not believe that God is the material cause of the Universe. Whereas the *Upanishads* propound that Brahman is the cause for creation; all are born from it and all die in it. Though it creates the universe, it is not exhausted by it.

Materialists, empiricists, behaviourists and classical physicists who believe in materialism emphasize that matter is the ultimate reality; which means that reality is conceived as a corporeal mass. For the materialists there is no "ultimate or absolute principle" which is the cause of all causes. Emerson strongly detested the philosophy of the materialists. He believed that a materialist could become an idealist, but not an idealist could ever think of becoming a materialist. He says: "The foundations of man are not in matter, but in the spirit,"[18] and again, "Spirit is the Creator. Spirit hath life in itself. And man in all ages and countries embodies it in his language as the Father."[19] Emerson was influenced by many idealistic traditions, more particularly the Vedantic philosophy shaped his vision and thought. He also drew inspiration from Plato's idealism. It cannot however be denied that Plato was influenced by the idealism of *Upanishads*. Therefore, Emerson's idealism became a blend of the *Upanishads* and Plato's. It was his firm conviction that Plato's fundamental concepts such as the complete independence of soul and body, the idea of good, immortality and the concept of fundamental unity were moulded by the "Upanishadic" idealism. Emerson writes: "The unity of Asia and the detail of Europe; . . . Plato came to join. . . . The excellence of Europe and Asia are in his brain."[20] Carpenter regarded Emerson's essay on "Plato" as "the kernel of Emerson's orientalism."[21] Emerson did not see Plato as an Oriental philosopher but considered him as a synthesis of "the infinitude of the Asiatic soul" and "the active and mature genius of Europe."

Emerson's aversion to materialism was strengthened by his reading of the *Upanishads* and the *Bhagvad Gita*. The story of Maitraya in *Brihadaranyaka Upanishad* who refuses to accept her share and prays to her husband Yajnavalkya to endow her with the knowledge of the Ultimate Reality must have deeply impressed Emerson. Similarly, he must have been deeply impressed by Charles Wilkins' translations[22] of *Sthitaprajna Yoga* which constitutes the last eighteen verses of the second chapter of the *Bhagvad Gita*. In these verses Krishna taught Arjuna on the battlefield as to how one should attain equanimity of mind.

The materialistic philosophy rejects all *a priori* considerations and emphasizes *a posteriori* considerations. It denies intuition as a means for knowing the ultimate truth. Emerson discarded this philosophy which does not take human mind into consideration. He wrote in "Nature": "Idealism saith: matter is a phenomenon, not a substance. Idealism acquaints us with the total disparity between the evidence of our own being and the evidence of the world's being. The one is perfect, the other, incapable of any assurances, the mind is a part of the nature of things; the world is a divine dream, from which we may presently awake to the glories and certainties of day."[23] Such a view is totally opposed to the materialistic emphasis of knowledge gained through sense organs. Emerson saw this fundamental difference between materialism and idealism and said:

> What is popularly called transcendentalism among us is idealism; Idealism as it appears in 1842. As thinkers, mankind have ever divided into two sects, Materialists and Idealists; the first class founding on experience, the second on consciousness; the first class beginning to think from the data of the senses, the second class perceive that the senses are not final, and say, the senses give us representations of things, but what are the things themselves, they cannot tell. The materialist insists on facts, on history, on the force of circumstances and the animal wants of man; the idealist on the power of Thought and Will, on inspiration, on miracle, on individual culture. These two modes of thinking are both natural, but the idealist contends that his way of thinking is in higher nature. He concedes all that the other affirms, admits the impressions of sense, admits their coherency, their use and beauty, and then asks the materialist for his grounds of assurance that things are as his senses represent them.[24]

Materialists consider the external world as real; whereas idealists as an appearance, hence, it has not substance of reality. Sankara conceived the world as unreal (*Jagat Mithya*). Influenced by this Vedantic concept, Emerson repudiates the materialistic view of the world as real: "the materialist takes his departure from the external world, and esteems a man as one product of that. The idealist takes his departure from his consciousness and reckons the world as appearance. The materialist respects sensible masses, society, government, social art and luxury, every establishment, every mass, whether majority of numbers, or extent of space, or amount of objects, every social action. The idealist has another measure which is metaphysical, namely, the rank which things themselves take in his consciousness; not at all the size or appearance."[25] In Buddhism also, we find an idealism which is identical with the Vedantic idealism. Emerson knew that Buddhism was idealistic nature when he wrote: "Buddhism is an expression of it."[26] *Vijanavada*, a branch of Buddhist philosophy, is transcendental and idealistic in nature.

From subjective idealism, Emerson moves to what Whicher calls "spirituality."[27] The last three sections of his essay "Nature" reveal his spiritualistic tendencies. Spirituality means that the Spirit which he calls as Over-Soul, of which the world is an effect, or a shadow, or an apparition, is the same as the self of man. Here, Emerson identifies himself as a true Vedantin.

Nature always speaks of Spirit. Emerson writes in "Spirit": "It suggests the absolute. It is a perpetual effect. It is a great shadow pointing always to the sun behind it."[28] Of this Spirit he again says: "We can foresee God in the coarse, and, as it were, distant phenomena of matter; but when we try to define and describe himself, both language and thought desert us, and we are helpless as fools and savages."[29] Idealism responds in the same manner that matter is a phenomenon, not a substance. In the *Bhagvad Gita*, this Spirit has been used as *Adhyatma* to mean the Supreme Soul:

> aksaram brahma paramam
> svabhavo dhyatmam veyate
> bhutabhavodbhavakaro
> visargah karmasamjnitah.[30]
>
> (The imperishable is Brahman, the Supreme, is dwelling in the individual body is called *Adhatma*. The offering which causes the origin of beings is called Karma).

This Brahman, as absolute cosmic principle, is the ultimate cause of universe. Soul and Nature are the manifestations of Brahman.

It is the power, the primal and eternal energy that lies behind all natural phenomena. It is the life force that pervades the whole universe and everything is illuminated by it. The mind being finite cannot measure the infinite which is immeasurable. However, it can be known intuitively, by negating everything. Brahman in the *Upanishads* is rightly regarded as silence. In the *Taitiriya Upanishad* (II.iv.1), it is described as: *Yatovaco nivartante, aprapya menasasaha*[31] (Brahman is that whence words return along with the mind, turn back frustrated). In the *Kena Upanishad* (II.3) a similar description is found: *na tatra caksur gacchati no vag gacchati no menah.*[32] (There the eye goes not, speech goes not, nor the mind; we know not, we understand not how one would teach it.)

The transcendental nature of Brahman is silence. Sri Aurobindo in his "The Life Divine" describes the nature of Ultimate Reality as "the transcendent silence."[33] In Buddhism also, the Ultimate Reality is described through silence of Buddha. Emerson also believed that the nature of the ultimate truth cannot be verbalized. In "Self-Reliance," he gives expression to such a view. For Emerson, like Vedantin or a Buddhist, the highest spiritual realization is possible through intuition and not intellect; and this realization defies communication through words. He remarks in his essay in "Self-Reliance": "And now at last the highest truth on this subject [self-reliance] remains unsaid; probably cannot be said; for all that we say is the far-off remembering of the intuition. The soul raised over passion beholds identity and eternal causation, perceives the self-existence of Truth and Right, and calms itself knowing that all things go well."[34] The "Over-Soul," Emerson calls it, "Wise silence." It is the silence of the highest experience. He reiterates the same view:

> Man is timid and apologetic; he is no longer upright; he dares not say, 'I think', 'I am', but quotes some saint or sage. He is ashamed before the blade of grass or the blowing rose. These roses under my window make no reference to former roses or to better ones; they are for what they are: they exist with God today. Therefore is not time to them. There is simply the rose; it is perfect in every

> moment of its existence. . . . But man postpones or remembers; he does not live in the present. . . . We shall not always set so great a price on a few texts, on a few lives.[35]

The four *mahavakyas* of the *Upanishads* such as *aham brahmasmi* (I am Brahman), *Tattvamasi* (Thou are that), *Ayamatma Brahma* (The self is Brahma) and *Prajnanam Brahma* (Brahma is consciousness) point out the essential oneness of the Universal Soul, as also, the individual soul. The "soul of the whole" which is the Universal Soul or Brahman is also present in man as individual soul. The transcendental spiritual power of the universe, the Over-Soul or Brahman when manifested in the individual in an immanent form is called *Atman*. When Emerson says: "within man is the soul of the whole; the wise silence; the Universal beauty, to which every part and particle is equally related; the eternal ONE,"[36] he means that each individual has in him the Over-Soul or *paramatman*. He asserts the identity of this Universal Spirit of man:

> We learn that the highest is present to the soul or man that the dread universal essence, which is not wisdom, or love, or beauty, or power, but all in one, and each entirely, is that for which all things exist, and that by which they are that spirit creates; that behind nature, throughout nature, spirit is present, one and not compound it does not act upon us from without, that is, in space and time, but spiritually, or through ourselves; therefore, that spirit, that is, the Supreme Being does not build up nature around us, but puts it forth through us, as the life of the tree puts forth new branches and leaves through the pores of the old. As a plant upon the earth, so a man rests upon the bosom of God; . . . and we learn that man has access to the entire mind of the Creator, is himself the creator in the finites.[37]

Thus the final vision is revealed in identification of the individual soul with Spirit, the oneness of the individual soul and the Universal Self. Sankara's position in this regard is not different. He finds unity in the 'Self'. All is one in Self; everything is contained in it. The phenomenal world is the product of the Self. Thus both Emerson and Sankara move from idealism to spirituality. Idealism denies reality outside; spirituality discovers reality inside. Emerson says: "The Idealist says, God paints the world around your soul. The spiritualist saith, yea, but (O) God is within you. The self of self creates the world through you."[38]

Emerson moves from idealism to spirituality precisely because the former does not satisfy the intense cravings of the inner heart. "The heart resists it [Idealism], because it balks the affections in denying substantive being the men and women. Nature is so pervaded with human life that there is something of humanity in all and in every particular. But this theory makes nature foreign to me, and does not account for that consanguinity which we acknowledge with it."[39] However, he has no contempt for the matter; he never parts with it but considers it essential to see the reality. By this very fact, he enjoys nature. He declares, "whether nature enjoys a substantial existence without, or is only the apocalypse of the mind, it is alike useful and alike venerable to me."[40] "I have no hostility to nature" he confesses in "Nature," "but a child's love. . . . I do not wish to fling stones at my beautiful mother nor soil my nest."[41] Moreover, nature for him is therapeutic; it heals man of his "impertinent griefs" and "mean egotism" as the first part of "Nature" amply illustrates. He writes: "Man's intercourse with heaven and earth becomes part of his daily food. In the presence of nature a wild delight runs through the man, in spite of real sorrows."[42] Sankara also does not make the world as totally unreal. He concedes a certain degree of reality to it. The world is neither "real" nor "unreal" because "of the non-real there is no coming to be; of the real there is no ceasing to be."[43] "Brahman is both undefined and defined; both are real"[44] (*Taitreya Upanishad*, II.Vi.1). "Brahman is immortal; things are actual"[45] (*Brihadaranyaka Upanishad*, I.vi.3). "External things are real"[46] (*Ibid*., II.i.20).

Emerson accepted idealism because of his contempt for matter, but because it "presents the world in precisely that view which is most desirable to the mind."[47] Idealism helped him see the world, as Sherman Paul points out "as the mediating agency between man and God."[48] Pollock observes that Idealism accepted by Emerson is a "highly unique position in its relation to the spiritual reality."[49] Thus, while accepting Idealism, Emerson moved to spirituality. Both Vedantic and Emerson's approach to reality is one and the same. Like Sankara, Emerson exhorted that the World can be subtracted only when knowledge dawns and not before. This makes us clear that one should humbly strive after true knowledge rather than engage in debates, discussions and quarrels.

NOTES

1. *Journals*, Vol. VII, pp. 120-30.
2. Whicher, *Freedom and Fate*, p. 53.
3. *Works*, Vol. I, p. 32.
4. *Journals*, Vol. IV, p. 282.
5. *Works*, Vol. VIII, p. 13.
6. *Works*, Vol. III, p. 211.
7. *Works*, Vol. III, p. 188.
8. *Works*, Vol. I, p. 53.
9. *Ibid.*, p. 49.
10. *Ibid.*, p. 33. "The Transcendentalist."
11. *Ibid.*, p. 61.
12. *Ibid.*, p. 58. "Nature."
13. *Works*, Vol. II, p. 274.
14. *The Thirteen Principal Upanishads*, p. 190.
15. *Ibid.*, p. 208.
16. *Ibid.*, p. 367.
17. *Works*, Vol. I, p. 60. "Nature."
18. *Ibid.*, p. 70.
19. *Ibid.*, p. 27.
20. *Works*, Vol. IV, p. 40. "Plato."
21. F.I. Carpenter, *Emerson and Asia*, p. 14.
22. "The Bhagvad-Gita," trans. Charles Wilkins, *American Transcendental Quarterly*, I, 20 (Fall 1973), p. 33. The translation of the verses which Emerson read runs as follows: "A man is said to be confirmed in wisdom when he forsake every desire which enter into his heart, and of himself is happy, and contented in himself. His mind is undisturbed in adversity, he is happy and contented in prosperity, and he is stronger to anxiety, fear, and anger. . . . The wisdom of that man is established, who in all things is without affection; and, having received good or evil, neither rejoiced at the

one, nor is cast down by the other. His wisdom is confirmed, when, like the tortoise, he can draw in all his members, and restrain them from their wonted purposes."

23. *Works*, Vol. I, p. 62. "Nature."
24. *Ibid.* pp. 329-30. "The Transcendentalist."
25. *Ibid.*, pp. 332-33.
26. *Ibid.*, p. 337.
27. Whicher, *Freedom and Fate*, p. 54.
28. *Works*, Vol. I, p. 63. "Nature."
29. *Ibid.*
30. *Bhagvad Gita*, pp. 452-53 (VIII:3).
31. *The Thirteen Principal Upanishads*, p. 285.
32. *Ibid.*, p. 335.
33. Sri Aurobindo, *The Life Divine* (Calcutta: Arya, 1930), p. 34.
34. *Works*, Vol. II, pp. 68-69. "Self-Reliance."
35. *Ibid.*, p. 67.
36. *Works*, Vol. II, p. 269. "The Over-Soul."
37. *Works*, Vol. I, pp. 63-64. "Nature."
38. *Journals*, Vol. IV, p. 78.
39. *Works*, Vol. I, p. 63. "Nature."
40. *Ibid.*, p. 53.
41. *Ibid.*, p. 59.
42. *Ibid.*, p. 9.
43. *Bhagvad Gita*, II. 16.
44. *The Thirteen Principal Upanishads*, p. 386.
45. *Ibid.*, p. 92.
46. *Ibid.*, p. 95.
47. *Works*, Vol. I, p. 59.
48. Sherman Paul, *Emerson's Angle of Vision* (Cambridge, Mass., 1952), p. 30.
49. "Ralph Waldo Emerson; the Single Vision," *American Classics Reconsidered*, p. 23.

Chapter V

Mysticism

Emerson's transcendentalism contains the fundamental idea of mysticism. Emerson was undoubtedly a mystic poet. He had mystical experiences and he recorded it in his journals, essays, and poems. After struggle and turmoil in his early years, he had his spiritual enlightenment in his later years. With his intense spiritual experience, Emerson spoke to the moral consciousness of man in or out of New England. He said, "the day of days, the great day of the feast of life, is that in which the inward eye opens to the unity in things, to the Omnipresence of law" and lamented "this beatitude . . . is not in us so much as we are in it."[1]

"Mysticism" is defined in various ways. According to *Encyclopedia Britannica,* it is generally defined as "any type of theory asserting the possibility of attaining knowledge or power through faith or spiritual insight."[2] Aldous Huxley regards mysticism as "the experience in which the subject and object relationship is transcended, in which there is sense of complete solidarity of the subject with other human beings and with the universe in general."[3] Abraham Maslow[4] says, "the whole universe is perceived as an integrated and unified whole." Such an experience can change one's life. The perceiver looks at things as they are in themselves. Such an insight, Maslow says, is like "godlike perception, superhuman perception." In other words, such experiences are "ego-transcending, self forgetful, egoless, unselfish." In such experiences the world is seen "only as beautiful god, desirable, worthwhile etc. and is never experienced as evil or undesirable." Evelyn Underhill has described mysticism as "the art of union with Reality. The mystic is the person who has attained that union in greater or less degree."[5] He contends that mysticism has four characteristics.[6] First, it is practical. Second, it is transcendental. The mystic elucidates, "the visible with the help of the invisible," he "knows God by common, and this direct intuition of the Absolute kills all lesser cravings." Third, the mystic is a lover. "Mystic love is a total dedication of the will; the deep-seated desire and tendency of the soul towards its source. It is a condition of humble access a life-movement of the self." Fourth, it entails a definite psychological experience. It is not merely a hunger of the heart, but "it involves the organizing of the whole self-conscious and unconscious."

William James says in his book, *The Varieties of Religious Experience: A Study in Human Nature*, that mystical experience is "ineffable." It defies expression; it cannot be imparted or transferred to others. He states the mystical state as the "poetic quality." In his view, the mystical experience is made to include the realm of all religious "faith and spiritual insight,"[7] and by this observation, Emerson was clearly a mystic. Emerson's mysticism, like that of many modern, Protestant writers from William Blake to Rufus Jones, was much less vague. Carpenter observes that Emerson was not a mystic like other sages, but merely a theoretical mystic who believed in the doctrine that "God, or the ultimate nature of reality, may be known in an immediate apprehension or insight," without experiencing the self-surrender of a practising mystic. But this observation can easily be refuted in the light of many spiritual experiences that Emerson himself had undergone in his lifetime which he recorded in his journals and essays. In his essay on "Nature," he has recorded his ascetic experience which is in true sense mystical. He writes: "Standing on the bare ground . . . my head bathed by the blithe air and uplifted into infinite space . . . all mean egotism vanishes. I became a transparent eyeball; I am nothing; I see all; the currents of the Universal Being circulate through me; I am part or parcel of god."[9]

This experience amply demonstrates that Emerson had mystical experience, that his ego was dissolved and merged with the

Universal Being. He became one and identified with the whole Universe. In another place, he writes; "A certain wandering light comes to me which I instantly perceive to the cause of causes." (*Journals*, IV, 248-49) In 1864, he lamented and asked himself for having had diminished experience: "Can we attend those enlargement and that intellectual elan which was a daily gift?" (*Journals*, X, 47) Thus Emerson did attain to a "variety of religious experience." And most important, he valued this experience above all others as it provided an insight into the conduct of life.

In the history of literature, Emerson belongs clearly to that type of mysticism, or mystical thought, which is distinctively occidental, protestant, and modern. Although he read widely in the mystical philosophy and poetry of the Orient and of Alexandria, he always disagreed with two of its traditional assumptions. First, he never exalted the mystical experience for its own sake as an end itself, as did Plotinus and the later Neo-Platonists. Second, he never agreed with the oriental conclusion that to the exclusive exaltation of the mystical experiences, all other active and partial experiences are valueless. Professor Rudolph Otto, whom Carpenter quotes approvingly, observes that Eastern mysticism is "static" and Western mysticism "dynamic" with the goal of Eastern as "the stilling of all *Karmani*, all works, all activity of will; it is quietism, *tyaga*, a surrender of the will and of doing."[10] This quietism and passivity in Eastern mysticism is misunderstood and misinterpreted. From the quietness and passivity springs the real action unattached to the results of consequences. Further, mysticism has universal characteristics and cannot be divided into such polar divisions and watertight compartments. Though Emerson disapproved of quietism the experience he had attained was led to by the metaphysical thinking done mostly in the light of Indian idealism and German Transcendentalism. In him verily "the twain do meet in the sympathies of the mystical bond, which is universal."[11] For Emerson, God was not a superhuman personal God but a state of consciousness and an absolute principle underlying the "Spiritual structure of the universe." William James remarks that "Emersoniasm . . . seems to let God evaporate into abstract Ideality."[12] Emerson's experience is identical with the experience of totality or the experience of the Brahman propounded in Vedantic mysticism.

Emerson rejected the fundamental conclusions of Catholic mysticism—that the perfect mystical experience is absolutely supernatural or superhuman, and therefore can never be achieved in this world. The official *Catholic Encyclopedia* declares that "the true ideal of Beatific Vision can only be reached in the next life."[13] But Emerson having read and acquainted with the writings of protestant mystics, such as Meister Eckhart and Jacob Bochme, taught that the mystical vision may be attained in this life and that man may therefore achieve perfection in this world. Because he described the mystical experience as natural rather than supernatural, Emerson's mysticism has often been condemned as "pantheistic" by Catholic and traditional critics.

Traditionally, the mystic realizes the personal inadequacy, passes through a period of "purgation" (sometimes called the "dark night of the soul") and finally arrives at "illumination" (or mystical experience). This final state may be known as "union with God," or having attained "knowledge of ultimate reality." Although Emerson did not suffer an absolutely "dark night of the soul," he did pass through a protracted period of personal suffering, combined with mental struggle and self-communion, reaching its "crisis" in 1832,[14] when he retired to the White Mountains and decided to resign his ministry. This period of "purgation" was followed by flashes of mystical insight, which he used these insights as the foundation of his book on "Nature." He developed the fundamental ideas of his philosophy from his natural experience which he described in the essay. In his essay on "The Over-Soul," he spoke again in the first person: "There is a depth in these brief moments which constrains us to ascribe more reality to them than to all other experiences."[15]

Clearly, Emerson did not use his mystical experiences for their own sake, but means to formulate ideas to be conveyed to the humanity. His mystical ideas, rather than his experiences themselves, are the significant elements in his "mysticism." He had the moments of "ecstasy." In this state, the soul seems to go beyond the body and to achieve identification with God: the individual transcends the limits of his individuality and feels himself part of the whole. The little self sees the Self in perspective, and shares the omniscience of God, or the Over-Soul. Therefore, all mystical ideas that spring from this state are not individualistic point of view but the point of view of God. In this sense, it is distinctly Vedantic in character.

Emerson believed that every human being is sustained by the same Divine power. One has to unfold one's own heart and discover the "Inner light" within. As an individualist he defended the soul's right to live by its dream of truth and power. According to Emerson, God is always waiting. He is waiting not only for man, the observer, but also and even more, for man the maker, the doer, the creator. He writers: "Every spirit builds itself a house, and beyond its house a world, and beyond its world a heaven. Know then the world exists for you. . . . What we are, that only can we see. All that Adam had, all that Ceaser could, you have and can do. . . . Build therefore your own world."[16]

He asserted that "the highest revelation is that God is in every man." (*Journals*, I, 335) He realized that "each mind lives in the Grand Mind, and everything teaches the infinitude of every man."[17] Emerson's faith in man's inherent divinity is clearly a rejection of the Calvinistic stress on natural depravity. This faith of Emerson expresses his optimism, which inheres in the certainty that "the Highest dwells with him; that the sources of nature are in his own mind."[18] "We live in succession, in division, in parts, in particles. Meantime within man is the soul of the whole; the wise silence, the universal beauty, to which every part and particle is equally related; the eternal ONE."[19] This consciousness of inner power is the key of his major doctrine—the belief in the "infinitude of the private man." (*Journals*, V, 380)

Based on this belief he maintained the power to master and direct circumstances by will and intellect; to relate and subordinate the natural facts to moral experience, to humanize knowledge and make it purposive and to use the material world as a symbol of the Spirit, to be read, interpreted and translated by insight into moral action. "For," he asserted in "The Poet," "we are not pans and barrows, not even porters of the fine and torch-bearers, but children of the fire."[20] The affirmative chord in Emerson's philosophy has a universal appeal to the consciousness of the capacity within man.

His intuitive ideas were mostly derived from the philosophical outlook of Quakerism, Neo-Platonic writers and Eastern writings. E.C. Stedman in his book, *Poets of America*, said that Emerson "refined and digested what was good in all philosophies."[21] He read Tuke's *Memoirs of the Life of Fox*, with considerable interest and found in him a kindred spirit. Both of them shared the view that religion should be based on an intuitive and personal experience, divorced altogether from hardened traditional forms and authority.

He also read the doctrines of Quakerism. Asked to define his religious position on one occasion he answered, "I am more a Quaker than anything else."[22] The Quaker's belief in the in-dwelling spirit of God and its all sufficiency as a guide to conduct is completely in accord with his convictions that each person is himself responsible for his present state and that everyone is his own friend or enemy. He exalted man's 'heart' and the religious sentiment above his reason, while he discarded the idea of Unitarians that the ultimate reliance of a human being must be on his own 'Mind'. Emerson resigned his ministry in 1832. He evolved a mysticism of the transcendental kind which emphasized on intuition and inner light.

Emerson also derived mysticism from Plato and Neo-Platonist mystical writers. As Carpenter[23] points out, Plato served two main functions for Emerson's mysticism: he was "the philosopher" and he was also "the mystic" who prepared Emerson's mind to receive the religious idealism of the Orient. His mysticism was derived from the Neo-Platonist mystical writers, Plotinus in particular. It was Plotinus who taught that the Supreme Good flows ceaselessly outward through Nature and flows back again into itself. The Platonian concept of emanation, of the "influx of the divine mind into our mind"[24] had contributed to the formation of Emerson's concept of the divine as the Over-Soul. Emerson believed that Ultimate Reality can be comprehended only by transcending the limitations of the physical senses and through intuition. He accepted the Platonic concept of "ecstasy," the mystical union of the human soul with the divine. These Neo-Platonic ideas were to a certain extent responsible for Emerson's radical individualism and his uncompromising insistence on self-reliance. It should also be noted that by "self" he meant the soul which receives the emanation from the Over-Soul, as his son clearly stated, it should more accurately have been called "God-Reliance." (*Journals*, VII, 456)

Though Emerson's mysticism is based on some of the doctrines of Unitarianism, Quaker faith and Neo-Platonism, it is undeniably influenced by Oriental thought. The idea that there is a single unifying principle of energy which is all pervasive and transcendental, and it can be realized through intuition is very much Hindu in tone and spirit. Emerson like any Orient mystic is not a philosopher in the Aristotelian sense; he is not concerned with a philosophical system to explain the world; rather he is a seeker of a way of salvation. His view of reality is not philosophic, but religious. The Being experienced by him in the words of Rudolf Otto is "valuable."[25] Emerson states in his "Introduction" to "Nature": "The foregoing generation beheld God and nature face to face; we through their eyes. Why should not we also enjoy an original relation to the universe? Why should not we have a poetry and philosophy an insight and not of tradition, and a religion by revelation to us and not the history of them."[26]

Emerson did not formulate any system. "I confess to a little distrust of that completeness of system which metaphysicians are apt to affect."[27] Further, he wrote, "A foolish consistency is the hobgoblin of little minds."[28] Again, "the moment it [logic] would appear as proposition and have separate value, it is worthless."[29] Although Sankara used "remorseless logic" to interpret *Sutra* and *Upanishads*, he meant to show that all the scriptures agree in holding Brahman to be the only worth.[30] Das Gupta points out that Sankara was not writing "a philosophy in the modern sense of the term, but giving us the whole truth as taught and revealed in the *Upanishads*." "Ultimate validity does not belong to reason but to the scriptures."[31]

His recordings in journals and essays reveal Emerson's Vedantic sense of mysticism. He writes: "There is a soul at the centre of nature and over the will of every man."[32] "Things are, and are not, at the same time. . . . All the Universe over, there is but one thing of which any proposition may be affirmed or denied."[33] In the *Upanishads* the idea of being and non-being is transcended and reconciled in the unconditioned and absolute Brahman. A similar passage is found in *Brihadaranyaka Upanishad* (II.iii.1)[34] where Brahman, the beyond (*tyam*) inexpressible, foundationless, unconscious, and unreal is contrasted with the universe which is being expressible, founded, conscious and real. The dialectic is further spelled out in *Chandogya Upanishad* (VIII.iii.5)[35] where the three syllables of *satyam—sa.ti* and *yam* are analysed. *Sa* stands for the immortal, *ti* for the mortal, and *Yam* for the meeting point of both. Emerson also says it is "neither being, nor essence, nor life, for it is above all these." (*Journals*, IV, 306) Emerson's vision of identity is found in "The Over-Soul": "Meantime within man is the soul of the whole: the wise silence; the universal beauty, to which every part and particle is equally related, the Eternal ONE. And this deep power in which we exist and whose beatitude is accessible to us, is not only self-sufficing and perfect in every hour, but the act of seeing and the thing seen, the seer and the spectacle, the subject and object, are one."[36] The ideas expressed in "Brahma" and "Hamatreya" are at once mystical and Advaitic Vedanta.

The mystical idea that Being transcends all phenomena involves two important conclusions: the unknowableness of Being and its supra personal character. Both Emerson and the Vedanta agree that the Absolute is unknowable. In "Experience" Emerson states that the First Cause refuses to be named, but man always tried to represent it by some symbol. These "quaint names" are "too narrow to cover this unbounded substance."[37] The ineffable nature of the Over-Soul is stated in "Nature": "Of that ineffable essence which we call spirit, he that thinks most, will say the least. We can foresee God in the coarse, and as it were, distant phenomena of matter; but when we try to define and describe himself, both language and thought desert us, and we are as helpless as fools and savages."[38] In his Essay on "Over-Soul," the same idea is represented: "Language cannot paint it with colours. It is too subtle. It is undefinable, unmeasurable, but we know that it pervades and contains us."[39] In his *Journal*, he observed: "What is God? We cannot say because he is unspeakable, the immeasurable, the perfect." (IV, 127)

Emerson agrees with the *Upanishads* and Sankara, when quoting Socrates in his essay "Swedenborg." "The teachings of the High Spirit are abstemious, and, in regard to particulars, negative. Socrates' genius did not advise him to act or find out but if he proposed to do somewhat not advantageous, it dissuaded him, 'what God is', he said, 'I know not; what he is not, I know.'"[40] The fact that Emerson denies personality to God, metaphysically his position is consistent with his conception of the Absolute. Spiritually, he had this experience. He writes in his essay, "Divinity School Address": "The Soul knows no person." For, if the Absolute is pure Being, incomprehensible, inexpressible, pure silence, attributing personality to it would veil and upset the very conception of Godhead. "Is God a person?" he questioned. "No, That is a contradiction. A person is finite. Personality is finiteness." (*Journals*, IV, 185) He justified in saying: "I feel there is some profanation in saying. He is personal. To represent him as an individual is to shut him out of my consciousness. He is then but a great man such as the crowd worships." (*Journals*, IV, 403-4)

In the realm of mystic experience, Emerson describes that all human thoughts will disappear and ultimately merge with God:

> Thought's holy light
> Better it is than gems or gold
> And Oh! It cannot die,

But thought will glow when the sun glows cold,
And mix with Deity. (*Thought*, ll. 4-8)

All thoughts vanish when man attains enlightenment because man is made in the image of God. Man, mind, nature and the world become one. He writes: "There is one mind common to all individual men. Every man is an inlet to the same and to all of the same."[41] "Each mind lives in the grand Mind, and everything teaches the infinitude of every man."[42]

"Good-Bye" depicts his mystic experience. The poet extremely vexed with the worldly life, wants to avoid the materialistic world because it does not satisfy his mystic perception:

Good-bye, proud world: I am going home:
Thou art not my friend, and I am not thine
Long through the weary crowds I roam;
A river-ask on the ocean clime,
Long I have been tossed like the driven foam;
But now, proud world: I am going home.[43]

The past is in search of spiritual joy. He realizes that the present world to which man is a slave cannot give it to him. He wants to transcend the earthly pleasures. He wants to choose a lonely spot where he can sit and contemplate upon God:

I am going to my own hearth-stone,
Bosomed in you green hills alone,—
A secret book in a pleasant land,
Whose groves the frolic fairies planned;
Where arches green, the live long day,
Echo the blackbird's round lay,
And vulgar feet have never trod
A spot that is sacred to thought and God.[44] (*Good-Bye*, ll. 15-22)

To attain communion with creation is his sole desire. Once he achieves that, the world full of evils and conceited people is nothing to him. To such an enlightened person, "there is no outside, no enclosing wall, no circumference." (*Journals*, VIII, 242) He expresses this idea eloquently in the last stanza:

O, when I am safe in my sylvan home,

I tread on the pride of Greece and Rome;
And when I am stretched beneath the pines,
Where the evening star so holy shines,
I laugh at the love and the pride of man,
At the sophist schools and the learned clan,
For what are they all, in their high conceit,
When man in the bush with God may meet?[45] (ll. 23-30)

Emerson's discovery of God becomes more evident in his poem "Self-Reliance." The symptom of the powerful emotional presence of God is intensely felt by the poet. Emerson's "Self-Reliance" was logical result of Protestant doctrine. The man who obeys the "Over-Soul" within himself needs the aid of no institution. "The relations of the soul to the divine spirit are so pure that it is profane to seek to interpose helps."[46] In the poem "Self-Reliance" he says:

I will be
Light-hearted as a bird, and herewith God,
I find him in the bottom of my heart,
I hear continually his voice therein.[47] (*Self-Reliance*, ll. 2-5)

The didactic tone and prophetic vision is more concretely projected in the last lines of the poem:

The little needle always knows the North
The little bird remembereth his note,
And his wise seer within me never em,
I never taught it what it teaches me,
I only follow, when I act aright.[48] (*Self-Reliance*, ll. 6-10)

This distinct philosophy transformed him into a leader of thought who would eventually be hailed in the famous words of Matthew Arnold, as "the friend and aider of all who would live in the spirit."[49]

Emerson expected that every individual should be self-reliant. He expected reformation in the near future. "The distinction of the new age" would be, he believed, "the refusal of authority." (*Journals*, IV, 495) There was a "steady tendency of the thoughtful and virtuous to a deeper belief and reliance on spiritual facts."[50] This gradual casting off of material side, and the growing trust in the private self-supplied powers of the individual was "the affirmative principle of the recent philosophy."[51] that "the next age will behold God in the ethical laws"[52] was his faith. In other words Emerson perceived that there would be a new revelation and a new race of men. Emerson sometimes assumed the air of John the Baptist prophesying a new Messiah. "The man who shall be born," he said, "whose advent men and events prepare and foresee, is one who shall enjoy his connection with a higher life."[53]

This mystical looking forward to a miraculous future was strengthened by Emerson's faith in America. For Emerson America meant freedom from all authority. "A nation of men will for the first time exist," he declared, "because each believes himself inspired by the Divine Soul which also inspires all men."[54] He believed that it would be the function of the United States to realize the spiritual religion of the future, and to embody the moral sentiment "in the jaws, in the jurisprudence, in international law, in political economy." (*Journals*, X, 144)

The idea that the world was an emanation from God was a doctrine which Emerson derived from Plotinus and found confirmation in Indian thought. "I believe," he said, "in the omnipresence; that is, that the All is in each particle; that entire nature reappears in every leaf and moss." (*Journals*, V, 184) Nobody can comprehend the nature and the power of God with normal faculties. Man must transcend his faculties in order to understand the divine power:

> The great Idea baffles wit,
> Language falters under it,
> It leaves the learned in the lurch;
> Nor art, nor power, nor toil can find
> The measure of the eternal Mind,
> Nor Hymn, nor prayer, nor church. (*The Bohemian Hymn*, ll. 7-12)

God was the "centripetal force in the depths of soul." (*Journals*, IV, 215) That man had divinity within himself in Plotinus and the Indians. He arrived at it by the way of the distinction between the 'Reason' and the 'Understanding' which he took from Coleridge. "Our compound nature," he said, "differences us from God; but our reason is not to be distinguished from the divine essence." (*Journals*, III, 235) Emerson considered this to be the most important feature of his philosophy. "In all my lectures," he said, "I have taught the doctrine, namely, the infinitude of the private man." (*Journals*, V, 380)

The idea of power of God is successfully carried out in his poem "The Informing Spirit," wherein Emerson clearly tells us that God is present in all creatures, big or small, wise or wicked. The difference lies in the degree of manifestation. He is omnipresent and all-powerful.

> There is no great and no small
> To the soul that maketh all:
> And where it cometh, all things are;
> And it cometh everywhere.
> I am the owner of the sphere,
> Of the seven stars and the solar year,
> Of Caesar's hand and Plato's brain,
> Of Lord Christ's heart, and Shakespeare's strain. (ll. 1-8)

The entire universe is pervaded by god. Emerson often wondered at the creation of stars, planets, the sky, clouds and the entire solar system. He himself said that the stars "were born heirs of the dome of God" (*Journals*, IV, 281) and that the stars were the last outpost of God's providence. "God be thanked," Emerson wrote of his own need for the heaven, "who set stars in the sky: planted their bright watch along the infinite deep and ordained such fine intelligence betwixt us and them." (*Journals*, IV, 47) The stars seemed to him to take beyond the horizon. "The blue zenith," he wrote, "is the point in which romance and reality meet."[55] And in astronomy he felt the visual promise of "everything"; the lawful heavens promised him successful moral navigation, and he took rightly walks under the stars to take his spiritual bearings." (*Journals*, VI, 187) By sighting the sun and stars, he hoped to find his latitude. In the contemplation of the stars he participated in their animating law: "I please himself rather with contemplating the penumbra of the thing than the thing itself" and he found that this referred him "to a higher state than I now occupy." (*Journals*, III, 197-98)

What distinguishes Emerson's mysticism is his attempt to apply his mystical ideas to the daily conduct of life. His emphasis on the supreme value of the mystical experience for the illumination and guidance of practical life in this world differs from Catholic mysticism. "The union with God" is common alike to the ancient Hindu scriptures, the German transcendental philosophers, and the more vaguely Romantic poets of Europe and America.

For Emerson, everything starts merely from the record of inner experiences, from the "I." The truth is that Emerson firmly believed in the inner light. According to him, every man must become self-reliant. By "self-reliance" Emerson meant obedience to the Over Soul. Man, he said, must surrender his individual will and intellect, and act only in obedience to the instincts of his soul. These instincts are Over Soul expressing itself in him. They are identical with the forces which govern the material universe. They are, therefore, moral and he who obeys them cannot do wrong. Man is great insofar as he makes himself a vehicle for the divine spirit. "As the traveller who has lost his way throws his reins on his horses' neck and trusts to the instinct of the animal to find his road, so must we do with the divine animal who carries us through this world."[56]

Religion is a self-surrender of the individual to something larger than himself. In traditional Christianity the individual surrenders to the city of God, whose earthly representative is the Church. The Church gave the individual moral standards which can be used by him to evaluate his own experiences. Emerson recommended that the individual should surrender to his own unconscious. "The unconscious," he said, "is ever the act of God Himself." (*Journals*, III, 325) By combining mysticism and Puritanism Emerson pointed out that the moral sentiment, the instincts of the individual, and the Over-Soul are all identical.

Emerson's experiences are akin to the experience of totality or the experience of the Brahman propounded in Vedantic mysticism. Emerson had a contemplative mind as opposed to the general Western ideal of activity. Though it is very difficult to say whether Emerson arrived at a mystic union with God or "an ineffable communion with the Over-Soul."[57] One can conclude by taking into account all his recordings in journals and writings that "his whole mental and spiritual attitude was mystical."[58] It was a mysticism of a purer kind where the emphasis was on experience and not simply on theory. Christy is of the opinion that "Emersonian thought was a matter of almost pure mysticism."[59] He goes on to say that "the plain man's *Weltanschauung* is artless and not speculative, based on common sense. That of Emerson, Thoreau and Alcott was the fruit of the mystical temperament and some metaphysical thinking, mixed with an unusual dash of the urbane." (*Ibid.*, p. 267)

NOTES

1. *Works*, Vol. I, p. 22. "Nature."
2. Evelyn Underhill and A.J. Pringle-Pattison, "Mysticism," *Encyclopedia Britannica*, Vol. XVI, p. 51.
3. Qtd. Robert Avens, "Mysticism: Essential for Survival," *New Catholic World*, 219, No. 1310 (1976), p. 69.
4. Abraham Maslow, *Religion Values and Peak Experiences*, pp. 59-68.
5. Evelyn Underhill, *Practical Mysticism* (1955), p. 5.
6. *Ibid.*, pp. 82-94.
7. William James, *The Varieties of Religious Experience*, p. 424.
8. The disagreement between the strict Catholic mystics and the broader Protestant mystics centres on the interpretation of the mystical experience as absolute and supernatural or as relative and natural.
9. *Works*, I, p. 10. "Nature.
10. Rudolph Otto, *Mysticism East and West* (New York, 1932), p. 32.
11. Arthur Christy, *The Orient in American Transcendentalism: A Study of Emerson, Thoreau and Alcott* (New York, 1932), p. 271.

12. William James, *The Varieties of Religious Experience* (New York, 1902), p. 32.
13. G.N. Sanvage, "Mysticism," *The Catholic Encyclopedia.*
14. Record in his *Journals*, Vol. II, pp. 491-503, entitled "Crisis."
15. *Works*, Vol. II, p. 267. "The Over-Soul."
16. *Works*, Vol. I, p. 79.
17. *Works*, Vol. X, p. 134.
18. *Works*, Vol. X, p. 107. "The Over-Soul."
19. *Ibid.*, p. 95.
20. *The Selected Writings of Ralph Waldo Emerson*, p. 320.
21. E.C. Steadman, *Poets of America* (Boston: Houghton Mifflin, 1885), pp. 158-59.
22. David G. Harkins, *Ralph Waldo Emerson—His Maternal Ancestors with Reminiscences of Him* (Boston, 1866), p. 48.
23. *Emerson Handbook*, p. 214.
24. *Ibid.*, p. 216.
25. Rudolf Otto, *Mysticism East and West*, p. 34.
26. *Works*, Vol. I, p. 3. "Introduction to Nature."
27. *Ibid.*, Vol. XII, p. 72.
28. *Ibid.*, Vol. II, p. 57.
29. *Ibid.*, Vol. II, p. 507.
30. *Indian Philosophy*, I, p. 445.
31. *A History of Indian Philosophy*, I, p. 435.
32. *Works*, Vol. II, p. 139.
33. *Ibid.*, Vol. III, p. 245.
34. *The Thirteen Principal Upanishads*, p. 97.
35. *Ibid.*, p. 265.
36. *Works*, Vol. II, p. 269.
37. *Ibid.*, Vol. II, p. 72-73. "Experience."
38. *Ibid.*, Vol. I, p. 62. "Nature."
39. *Ibid.*, Vol. II, p. 271. "The Over-Soul."
40. *Works*, Vol. IV, pp. 139-40. "Swedenborg."
41. *Works*, Vol. II, p. 9.
42. *Ibid.*, p. 12.
43. *The Selected Writings of Ralph Waldo Emerson*, p. 761.
44. *Ibid.*
45. *Selected Writings of Ralph Waldo Emerson*, p. 767.
46. *Essays*. Vol. I, p. 66.
47. *Selected Writings of Ralph Waldo Emerson*, p. 815.
48. *Ibid.*

49. Matthew Arnold, *Discourses in America* (New York, 1924).
50. *Essays*, Vol. II, p. 242.
51. *Ibid.*, p. 247.
52. *Works*, Vol. X, p. 222.
53. *Essays*, Vol. II, p. 268.
54. *Works*, Vol. I, p. 115.
55. *Works*, Vol. III, p. 172.
56. *Essays*, Vol. II, p. 31.
57. P.F. Quin, "Emerson and Mysticism," *American Literature*, XXI (Jan. 1950), p. 399.
58. Leyla Goren, "Elements of Brahminism in Transcendentalism of Emerson," *The Emerson Society Quarterly*, 34 (1 qtr. 1964), p. 8.
59. Arthur Christy, *The Orient in American Transcendentalism: A Study of Emerson, Thoreau and Alcott*, p. 266.

Chapter VI

Revaluation

Transcendentalism flourished as a major literary movement in New England from 1830 to 1860. The New England Transcendentalists comprising R.W. Emerson, H.D. Thoreau, Amos Bronson Alcott, George Ripley, Orestes Brownson, William Henry Channing, Samuel Johnson and Moncure Caniel Conway marked the third major phase of early American philosophy. Just as obedience to the will of God defined the purpose of Puritanism, and allegiance to a rule of reason and human freedom defined the purpose of the Enlightenment, so self-reliance or the assertion of man's unfettered allegiance to himself defines the meaning of Transcendentalism. By the early 1830s, the transcendentalists had brought a poetic, highly romantic focus to the problem of the meaning and purpose of man's life.

The period of transcendentalism was a period of renaissance in American thought and literature when the transcendentalists assimilated the thoughts and philosophy of other cultures and gave a new poetic philosophy to the American society. Therefore, transcendentalism is both a philosophical tradition and an American intellectual movement. Transcendentalism asserts that "man has something besides the body of flesh, a spiritual body, with senses to perceive what is true, and right and beautiful and a natural love for these, as the body for its food."[1] Emerson was the chief spokesman of this movement who "scouted the trial that the others were to follow."[2]

The immediate sources of Transcendentalism were the English romanticists like Coleridge and Wordsworth, the revival of Greek literature and the classics, Oriental mysticism and their own meditations on life and fondness for nature and the beauties of the great outdoors. All of these sources conspired to a unity for Emerson and other transcendentalists; each taught that man is essentially a poet, and the world simply an appearance for the individual soul or mind. They dealt with the fundamental issues of human life such as the nature of the universe, the nature of man and his place in the universe, the nature of good and evil, and man's duty to himself and to his fellow beings. They were highly characterized by their idealism, spirituality and mysticism. They interpreted reality in terms of idealism and romanticism and opposed all types of materialism and industrialism. They emphasized a return to nature somewhat in a Rousseaustic sense. They saw in nature a manifestation of the Supreme Spirit of the Universe. This pantheistic idea inherent in their attitude is identical with the Hindu thought which says that there is a Supreme Reality which animates both the being and non-being, and that man can realize this by destroying his ignorance. Their philosophy was also a revolt against John Locke's empiricism, materialism and sensationalism. They also opposed many of the basic tenets of Christianity. They believed in the potentiality of human nature and rejected the idea of sin and guilt. They also opposed the Puritanic denial of life based on arid asceticism in favour of a healthy enjoyment of life in the midst of nature.

Ralph Waldo Emerson had a greater effect not only on the minds of American but also on the whole humanity than any other thinker. For countless Americans he was the source of inspiration and the prophet of unbounded aspirations and hope for man. He did not possess the systematic mind and argumentative skill of Jonathan Edwards, nor the vigorous inventiveness, enterprise, and statesmanship of Thomas Jefferson. He could neither identify himself with a particular religious movement or sect nor become part of any particular political movement or social reconstruction. He did not formulate any philosophy or a doctrine to be imitated and cultivated. Rather Emerson found all genuine values and ideas within the infinitely rich poetic imagination or genius of man.

Born in Boston in 1803, Emerson was descended from several generations of Protestant clergyman. He was educated at Harvard in 1829 and accepted a pulpit in the Second Unitarian Church of Boston. However, by 1832 he resigned his position as a minister because of growing awareness in him that man is a spiritual being, that man can discover his true nature not through orthodox beliefs and institutions and creeds but through intuitive experiences. Thereafter, with these deep inner convictions and faiths, he travelled, lectured, and wrote and thus became a notable leader in the flowering literary activity in New England. He became the acknowledged leader of New England transcendentalism or romanticism. As poet, critic and lecturer, he was throughout his long life the untiring prophet of the creative genius and divinity of all mankind.

Emerson breathed a new and essentially romantic meaning into "transcendentalism" which he borrowed from Kant. Following the tradition of English romanticists, Emerson used "intuition" to signify the poetic faculty of seeing things creatively and seeing things with a freshness and richness. He wrote: "The sensual man conforms thoughts to things; the poet conforms things to his thoughts."[3] The post, because of his creatures, is by nature of transcendentalist or idealist, since he is truly self-reliant. Rather than conform his ideas to things, he makes things conform to his ideas. The poet makes his vistas or world from his imagination, or from the institutions of the mind itself. "The Imagination may be defined to be the use which the Reason makes of the material world."[4] Here Emerson implies the identity of imagination, reason, and intuition. Intuition suggests a direct seeing by the mind, reason connotes a comprehension of knowing by the mind, and imagination suggests a fabrication creating of things known.

Emerson's transcendentalism is therefore simply "romantic idealism." He says: "What is popularly called Transcendentalism among us, is Idealism; Idealism as it appears in 1842."[5] For Emerson, romantic idealism implies both a fresh and comprehensive outlook on all things. Religiously, it implies pantheism; morally, it implies self-reliance or individualism; and, as an outlook on nature and society as well, it signifies spirituality or mysticism. Pantheism rejects both theism and deism. It finds divine life in all things—in nature, in man—since all are, in a poetic sense, infinitely rich and inexhaustible.

According to Emerson common sense or ordinary reason is too limited, too mundane, for true religions aspirations. Religion, for Emerson, must uphold the divinity or self-sufficiency of the soul itself, since the soul is the source of all perspectives. It is through the intuitive powers of men's souls that the divine and the moral reality finds a unity. The more self-reliant or self-existent a soul is, the more divine it is. The more self-reliant or integrity-bound it is, the more it aspires to the highest moral goals. True individuality, for Emerson, means fullness of self, a realization of the infinite universal self. The more truly individual a man is, the more he is a whole man, a harmony of complementary parts. Emerson ultimately indicates the mystical turn of his thought. Mysticism not only involves the assertion that the soul of man and the divine reality are capable of union or oneness, it also involves the assertions that both are infinite or essentially without limitation, and that the achievement of oneness is possible only through intuition or direct knowledge of the truth. It is in this sense that Emerson stands as the best exponent of transcendentalism, not merely because he formulated its ideology more coherently than any other romantic, but by the manner in which he succeeded in exhibiting, simply and poetically, the inspiring character of the transcendental position. He goaded the ordinary man with enthusiasm to discover his own unbounded greatness and worth. He not only emphasized self-reliance, an essential of transcendental doctrine, but also united it with a complete scheme of values for man that combined religion, morality, nature, and society. He brought transcendentalism "out into the world" in such a way as to teach a wider audience than any other transcendentalist.

Emerson was greatly indebted to the Hindu mystical writings, particularly to the *Upanishads* and the *Bhagvad Gita*. His assertion that man has ideas "that come not through the five senses, or the powers of reasoning; but are either the result of direct revelation from God, his immediate inspiration, or his immanent presence in the spiritual world," and that "man has something besides the body of flesh, a spiritual body, with senses to perceive what is true, and right and beautiful, and a natural love for these, as the body for its food"[6] is very akin to the Vedantic thought and philosophy. He found idealism and spirituality in the Orient. For Emerson the mystical experiences and ideas of the great Indian mystics were always confounding and deeply fascinating. He admired the Vedantic literature because it advocated a life in harmony with the laws of nature. His immense love of nature has long been established in his poetry and writings. His love for nature was delicate and passionate. He believed that nature was God's world with its contribution of solace, spiritual ecstasy and reverent faith. He always regarded himself as naturalist. He writes: "Here we are impressed with the inexhaustible riches of nature. The universe is a more amazing puzzle than ever as you glance along this bewildering series of animated forms—the hazy butterflies, the carved shells, the birds, beasts, fishes, insects, snakes and the upheaving principle of life everywhere incipient, in the very rock aging organized forms."[7] Nature gave him abundant happiness, knowledge and wisdom. He did not merely admire the beauty of nature. He believed that a really enlightened person derives joy as well as wisdom from it. He remarked:

> Nature never wears a mean appearance. Neither does the wisest man extort her secret, and lose his curiosity by finding out all her perfection. Nature never became a toy to a wise spirit. The flowers, the animals, the mountains reflected the wisdom of his best hour, as much as they had delighted the simplicity of his childhood.[8]

In his essays and addresses Emerson referred to nature in order to indicate the close relationship between nature and human nature and drive home his arguments, thoughts and ideas. He writes: "I am the lover of uncontained and immortal beauty. In the wilderness, I find something more dear and connate than in streets or villages. In the tranquil landscape and especially in the distant line of the horizon, man beholds somewhat as beautiful as his own nature."[9] Even during his European tour, he used to retire to the woods and listen to the sweet songs of the birds. He wrote: "I go out daily and nightly to feed my eyes on the horizon and the sky, and come to feel the want of this scope as I do of water for my washing."[10] After his return from Europe, Emerson had an ambition to publish an essay on Nature. He himself said in his *Journals*: "I think I must do these eyes of mine the injustice to write a new chapter on Nature."[11] He fulfilled his ambition when he wrote a beautiful essay on nature and published it in 1836.

Emerson always craved for Oriental metaphors and illustrations and he employed the Oriental writings pregnant with wise and witty sayings and proverbs in his writings in order to strengthen his arguments.[12] In his essay on "Books," he gave high praise to the sacred books of the East. They are: "*The Desatir of the Persian and the Zoroastrian Oracles*; the *Vedas* and *Laws of Manu*; the *Upanishads*, the *Vishnu Purana*, the *Bhagvad Gita* of the Hindus, the books of the Buddhists."[13] Referring to this Oriental Eldorado, he wrote: "All these books are the majestic expressions of the universal conscience, and are more to our daily purpose than this year's almanac or this day's newspaper. But they are for the closest, and to be read on the bended knees. Their communications are not to be given or taken with the lips and the end of the tongue, but out of the cheek, and with the throbbing heart."[14] In his *Journals*, he had written: "I think Hindoo books are excellent gymnastic for the mind."[15] But the one book which received unusual praise and attention from Emerson was the *Bhagvad Gita*. "I owed—my friends and I owed—a magnificent day to the *Bhagvad Gita*. It was the first of books; it was as if an empire spoke to us, nothing small or unworthy, but large, serene, consistent, the voice of an old intelligence which in another age and climate had pondered and thus disposed of the same questions which exercise us."[16]

Emerson himself had felt his spiritual inclination and affinity towards the Hindus. He admitted his indebtedness to Vedantic thought in unambiguous terms. After reading "A Hymn to Narayana," he wrote to his aunt Marry on June 10, 1822: "I am curious to read your Hindu mythologies. One is apt to lament over indolence and ignorance, when we read some of those sanguine students of the Eastern antiquities, who seem to think that all the books of knowledge, and all the wisdom of Europe twice told, lie hidden in the treasures of the Brahmins."[17] the concept of Over-Soul, in all probability, was conceived by his reading of the *Bhagvad Gita* where the Supreme Spirit is called *Adhyatman* or *paramatman*.

The mystic description of the Ultimate Reality in the *Upanishads* (*neti, neti*, not this, not this) had deeply influenced Emerson. The nature of Ultimate Reality cannot be grasped by the mind which is finite and limited. The mind can only operate in the field of the known. Therefore, the process of arriving at the Ultimate reality involves the denial of whatever is known by the mind. By discarding the false one after another (through negation, *neti, neti*) one may eventually reach the highest state of no-mind.

Like the concept of "neti," the concept of "Maya" or illusion also influenced Emerson a great deal. "Maya" means that Brahman is the only ultimate reality and the phenomenal world is not ultimately real; or in other words, it has not *paramarthika satta.* This is embodied in Sankara's well-known verse: *Brahma Satya Jagan mithya Jiva Brahmaiva Napara* which means Brahman is the truth and the world is illusion, and the undivided self is the part of the Brahman. Emerson conveyed the same idea in his essay on "Illusion" and the poem "Maia."

> Illusion works impenetrable,
> Weaving web innumerable.
> Her gay pictures never fail,
> Crowds each on other, veil on veil,
> Charmer who will be believed
> By man who thirsts to be deceived.[18]

In 1861, he wrote in his *Journals* about the Maya of Vishnu.[19] In another context he wrote that the world is born of Maya.[20] The poem "Hamatreya" also seems to have been influenced by the concept of Maya.[21] In his essay on "Illusion," he wrote: "I find men victims of illusion in all parts of life. Children, youths, adults, and old men, all are led by one bauble or another. Yoganidra, the goddess of illusion, Proteus or Mormus, or Glifis Mocking,—for the power has many names,—is stronger than the Titans, stronger than Apollo."[22] Emerson's firm conviction is that the *maya* is a power by which the Over-Soul or Brahman creates the phenomenal world. He remarks "God is a reality and his method is illusion."[23] This idea is elaborately described by Emerson in his *Journals*: "Maya [Illusion] of the Hindoos, Rudra says, O thou, who always unalterable, creates, conservest, and destroyest this universe, by the aid of Maya, that energy in numerous forms which . . . makes believe that it is distinct from these, and gives to the world an apparent reality. Maya. . . . The Veda says: 'The world is born of Maya.' '*Brahma' qui 'n' a pas de qualities*."[24] All his recordings and writings demonstrate that he had a comprehensive understanding of the conception of the Vedantic idea of *Maya.*

Like the concept of *Maya*, the law of *Karma* is also related to the doctrine of rebirth, transmigration of the soul and the principle of good and evil. The law of *Karma* has been discussed in the *Satpatha Brahmana* and in the *Upanishads*. Its fundamental point is that human action is never wasted. Virtue is rewarded, and vice is punished. It is the moral foundation of the universe and can be called the law of moral retribution. *Karma* implies that every action has its counter-reaction. Based on the immutable principle of cause and effect, this Law accounts for the cause of every individual and human event including suffering and joy. According to the *Upanishads* nothing happens through chance or coincidence, whatever happens is determined by *Karma* of this life or *Karma* of the past life. The fruit of right *Karma* which must have its effect without our foreknowledge is called fate or destiny.

Emerson accepts the law of *Karma* in general but does not seem to accept its deterministic aspect. He wrote in his *Journals*: "As long as I am weak, I shall talk of Fate; whenever the God fills me with his fullness, I shall see the disappearance of Fate."[25] His essay "Fate" also contains his negative attitude which was influenced by Hindu, Greek and Mohammedan ideas. His reading of the "Code of Manu" enabled him to share this fundamental Hindu belief. The doctrine of Compensation, discussed in his essay "Compensation," bears ample testimony to this.

Karma and rebirth or transmigration are two integrated principles. With this is also associated the idea of immortality (*nityatva*). Soul, being immortal, does not die with the death of an individual. The sum total of one's good and bad *karma* remains tied with the *jivatma* or individual soul in a very subtle form. When a person realizes the Brahman, he becomes freed forever from the cycle of *karma* and death and never experiences transmigration. Accepting this law, Emerson wrote in his essay on "Compensation": "You cannot do wrong without suffering wrong."[26] "Every secret is told, every crime is punished, every virtue rewarded, every wrong redressed, in silence and certainty. What we call retribution is the universal necessity by which the whole appears wherever a part appears."[27] In another essay "Worship," he says that every service is rewarded: "He is great, whose eyes are opened to see that the reward of actions cannot be escaped, because he is transformed into his action, and taketh its nature."[28] Buddhism also believes in this doctrine and Emerson quotes Buddhist doctrine of *karma* in his essays "Worship" and "The Transcendentalist." He writes: "The Buddhists say, 'no seed will die', every seed will grow. Where is the service which can escape its remuneration."[29] "The Buddhist, who thanks no man who says, "Do not flatter your benefactors, but who, in his conviction that every good deed can by no possibility escape its reward, will not deceive the benefactor by pretending that he has done more than he should, is a Transcendentalist."[30]

In the beginning Emerson believed in the individual immortality, but later he gave it up. He writes: "I confess that everything connected with our personality fails. Nature never spares the individual."[31] His rejection of individual immortality amounts to be his acceptance of immortality of soul. Like the Christians and Vedantists, he believed in the continuity of life. Emerson's conviction of this is unmistakable. He writes: "I believe in this life. I believe it continues."[32] It suggests that Emerson believed in the continuity of life. He records: "Travelling the path of life through thousands of births."[33] He further remarks, "that all things subsist, and do not die, but only retire a little for right and afterwards return again."[34]

The concepts of pantheism and mysticism are inherent in his philosophy. In the *Isa Upanishad*, the universe is conceived as a manifestation of God, *Isa vasyam idam sarvam yet kim ca jagatyam jagat*. It means that the entire universe is manifestation of God. Emerson conveys a similar idea. "The world proceeds from the same spirit as the body of man. It is a remoter and inferior incarnation of God, a projection of God in the unconscious."[35] An important corollary of pantheistic belief is that everything in nature including man is a miniature of Cosmic. Man is the microcosm of the macrocosm of the universe. This concept is fundamental to Emerson's pantheism.

Mysticism is another aspect common to Emerson and Indian thinkers. In the Vedanta, Buddhism and Taoism, mysticism is more or less described as an egoless state in which the person experiences the totality of the whole universe and becomes one with the universe. In this experience, as Carpenter describes: "the soul seems to go beyond the body and to achieve identification with God: the individual transcends the limits of his individuality and feels himself part of the whole."[36] And dualism ceases in this state and the person experiences *Samadhi* or *nirvana* or a state of Bliss. The mystic in such a state feels that the universe is not a creation distinct from God. God is the universe, and the universe is God. The *Mandukya Upanishad* emphasizes this point by saying that all is Brahman and Brahman is all. Emerson had this kind of experience on more than one occasion. He wrote: "Standing on the bare ground my head bathed by the blithe air, and uplifted into infinite space—all egotism vanishes. I become a transparent eye-ball, I am nothing. I see nothing; I see all the currents of the Universal Being circulate through me; I am part or particle of God."[37] In characteristic manner he has added, "there the mind integrates itself again. The attention which had been distracted into parts, is reunited, reinspired. The whole of nature addresses itself to the whole man. . . . It is more than a medicine, it is health."[38]

Emerson realized that in nature one can unfold one's own heart and discover God. He wrote: "The imaginative faculty of the soul must be fed with objects immense and eternal."[39] He perceived in nature "the true outline of the world,"[40] and the astonishment of landscape was "the meeting of the sky and the earth."[41] Here is the mystic line, the visible symbol in nature itself of the dualism of the universe. He recorded that "nature carries every integral part out to the horizon, and mirrors yourself to you in the universe."[42] A landscape—"a long vista in woods, trees on the shore of a lake coming quite down to the water, a long reach in a river, a double or triple row of uplands or mountains seen one over the other,"[43] rewarded Emerson not only with first sight, but with second sight and insight.

Further, he wrote, "we come into our own and make friends with matter,"[44] and he significantly added, "the greatest delight which the fields and woods minister, is the suggestion of an occult relation between man and the vegetable . . . [and] the power to produce this delight does not reside in nature, but in man, or in harmony of both."[45] This harmony can only be felt according to him through "the inexhaustibleness of imagination."[46]

In the process of spiritual experience, nature is instrumental both as the activator of insight and as the object of forms. Although man is dependent on nature, man is "absolutely, imperially free."[47] Emerson meant by it a freedom of perception. He gave undue importance to the perception of objects. But the freedom of perception has to travel beyond the awareness of the benefits of nature. "Man," Emerson added, "is not designed to be an idle eye before which nature pauses in review, but by his action is enabled to learn the irresistible properties of moral nature, perceived dimly by the mind of laws difficult to be grasped or defined yet everywhere working out their inevitable results in human affairs."[48] Freedom is only to be found in the perception of the correspondence of the physical and moral laws. Through freedom the insight is known. But this insight has to end in a message. The freedom of intuition demanded the necessity of precise form. The poet always experiences this insight. Therefore, he has a message to convey. "The poet," wrote Emerson, "who shall use nature as his hieroglyph must have an adequate message to convey thereby."[49] Emerson, as a poet, proclaimed the message of his intense spiritual experience and the most profound truth that God is one and He is found in all, to his fellow Americans.

For Emerson, there is not antithesis between practical and theoretical, between the humanistic and the scientific, between religion and science, between value and fact, between man and nature, between character and event. Man is one, mind is one, the nature is one, the world is one. He affirmed the oneness of God, for there is single order, one set of laws that operates for man as well as in the laboratory, in the mind as well as in the body. "There is no mind common to all individual men. Every man is an inlet to the same and to all of the same."[50] Man is face to face with God every hour because man is made in the image of God, which means that ideals are as natural to man as feathers are to birds. Emerson appeals to every young man "to become brave and upright man, who must find or cut a straight road to everything excellent."[51]

"Each mind in the grand Mind and everything teaches the infinitude of every man."[52] Keeping this in view, Emerson devalued the past and tradition and emphasized the right of each man to trust himself. "He who contemplates hath days without nights."[53] Emerson asserted that the harmony of man and the universe is with man as it is with God. "There is no outside, no enclosing wall, no circumference to us."[54]

Emerson was a great optimist. He believed that a day would come when all men would surrender to the Over-Soul.[55] He said that man must become self-reliant. By "Self-Reliance," Emerson meant obedience to the Over-Soul. Man, he said, must surrender his individual will and intellect and act only in obedience to the instincts of his soul, these instincts are the Over-Soul expressing itself in him, and are identical with the forces which govern the material universe; they are therefore, moral, and he who obeyed them could do no wrong. Man is great insofar as he makes himself a vehicle for the divine spirit. Emerson declared in the most uncompromising terms, "as the traveller who has lost his way throws his reins on his horse's neck and trusts to the instinct of the animal to find his road, so must we do with the divine animal who carries us through this world."[56]

For Emerson, faith is not a body of concepts or propositions; faith is not an intellectual system, but life, being or becoming. Faith is the quality of the whole person, an inwardness, which can never be conceived, analysed and communicated. His faith, like Kierkegaard's, is existential rather than cognitive, or logical or intellectual. Ronald F. Lee says, "Faith as he [Emerson] saw it was not mere belief in doctrine; nor was the ethical life a grudging adherence to a set of restrictions imposed upon one's natural impulses. Faith is the unsayable relation to the primary facts, and its principal mark is the transformation of person . . . religious faith is almost incommunicable because it is a condition that one knows only by being in it."[57] Communicating a condition or life is, Emerson says, like "the gnat grasping the world. All these exhaustive theories appear indeed a false and vain attempt to introvert and analyse the Primal Thought. That is upstream, and what is stress: Can you swim up the Niagara Falls?"[58]

If Faith is "being," Emerson observes, one cannot receive it from others. For "it is an intuition. It cannot be received second hand. Truly speaking, it is not instruction, but provocation, what I can receive from another soul. What he announces, I must find true in me, or reject; and on his word, or as his second, be he who he may, I can accept nothing."[59] He further states: "Faith is renouncing of oneself and coming to himself."[60] The absence of it as he says is degradation. It cannot be based on authority and tradition. "The faith that stands on authority is not faith. The reliance on authority measures the decline of religious, the withdrawal of the soul."[61]

Emerson observed all institutions, dogmas, traditions and beliefs are relatively unimportant. The inflexible dogmas kill the spirit. He regarded Christ as a human being; he was only for inspiration. He said, "by his holy thoughts, Jesus serves us, and then only."[62] But historical Christianity has attributed divine nature to him and denied it to the vast. "Once man was all," Emerson wrote, "now he is an appendage, a nuisance. And because the indwelling Supreme Spirit cannot wholly be got rid of, the doctrine of it suffers this perversion, that the divine nature is attributed to one or two persons, and denied to all the rest and denied with fury."[63] The obnoxious exaggeration of the 'Person' of Jesus to the extent of neglecting what he stood for, Emerson calls the main defect of historical Christianity. Emerson says, Jesus saw that God incarnates himself in man; he saw the mysteries of the soul. But the doctrinal foundations of Christianity distorted the message of Jesus. "But what a distortion did his doctrine and memory suffer in the same, in the next, and following ages"; Emerson wrote, "churches are not built on his principles, but on his tropes. Christianity became a Mythus"[64] Thus, Emerson believed that "the exaggeration of the personal, the positive, the ritual," corrupts all attempts to communicate religion."[65]

Emerson lamented: "There is faith in chemistry, in meat, and wine, in wealth, in machinery, in the steam engine, galvanic battery, turbine-wheels, sewing machines, and in public opinion, but not in divine causes."[66] The Western civilization, he believed, is more mechanical than spiritual, more political than religious, more desirous of power than peace. It is evident from the wars and the advancement of science and technology that the materialistic civilization has failed to bring happiness and peace to mankind. Far from promoting love and brotherhood, the world has been torn asunder by the illegitimate ambitions, jealousy, egotism, discord and bloodshed. Emerson found for this Western disease in the Oriental thought and wisdom. The Oriental mind has always given humanity great ideals and virtues; and tended to the largeness of heart. Buddhism, Hinduism and Jainism are an expression of it. In *English Traits*, the least Oriental of Emerson's volumes, he wrote: "For a self-conceited modish life, made up of trifles, clinging to a corporeal civilization, hating ideas, there is no remedy like the Oriental largeness."[67]

The modern man is thus "unmanned" and "metamorphosed into a thing."[68] Emerson observed that the church services are irrelevant. These are more human institutions wherein God in reality cannot be realized. "The prayers and even the dogmas of our church," Emerson wrote, "are like the Zodiac of Dauderah and the astronomical monuments of the Hindoos, wholly insulated from anything now extant in the life and business of people."[69] It must be clearly understood that Emerson had no quarrel with the Christian religion. "I agree with them," he said, "more than I disagree, I agree with their heart and motive; my discontent is with their limitations and surface and language."[70] Emerson never liked to attack the beliefs and sentiments of the others. But, according to him, they were to be displaced when higher ones were given. "True genius," he observed, "will not impoverish, but will liberate."[71]

Emerson realized that the answer for ills and evils in the society does not lie in machines or religious institutions or rituals, but in the realization that God is immediately present to every person. Man must realize this, and it is only in such realization that man can find peace and happiness. This is the heart of religion of Emerson and Sankara and scores of other Oriental mystics. "That which shows God in me fortifies me. That which shows God out of me, makes me a wart and wen."[72] Emerson asserted: "It is the office of a true teacher to show us that God is, not was; that He speaketh, not spoke."[73]

Emerson holds that man is wiser than he knows himself. The wisdom of man is intuitive or self-taught. Emerson was not a reformer from outside; but he believed that a reformer must begin by finding himself. He remained a mystic and moral optimist throughout his life, holding that the more men rely upon their individual souls, the more they will find universal harmony, beauty, and peace. His optimism is not based on chance or circumstances or a denial of unpleasant facts. Fate, necessity, and disaster according to him must all be included in the large infinite whole of reality.

Emerson succeeded in spreading the doctrine of intuition and self-reliance and in reaching a very wide audience. He stands as the finest representative of his age and has indeed outlived his age through his untiring célebration of the spiritual dignity of man. He spoke to all men, but from what he believed was original, direct insight. He did not convince them with arguments or experiments. He did not use any methods. He did not prove anything, nor did he venture any likely hypothesis; he simply presented his insights with sincerity and poetic beauty. Virtually all that Edwards claimed for God, Emerson claimed for the spiritual genius in every man. Like Jefferson, he was an optimist about human nature, believing that men had an innate sense of justice which could win over wrong. But he was at heart a metaphysical poet. Like Jefferson, he had no taste for Calvinism. But unlike Jefferson, he had an insatiable taste for the eternal and the infinite. Emerson found the supernatural in the natural, the metaphysical in the physical.

Emerson's impact and influence on American intellectual life is great and wide. Though his impact on Thoreau, Whitman, Hawthorne and others was noteworthy, he wanted no followers. He encouraged every one to be self-reliant. Though he has been criticized for borrowing ideas from Plato, Kant and many other Oriental thinkers as he found them inspiring, he is still regarded as the purest and greatest philosopher that America has produced. He firmly believed that the ideas of great philosophers could be grasped intuitively by the mind—by insight without extended reasoning. He used the name "transcendentalism" to teach the view that truth is directly revealed to every man if man will only turn within and become truly self-reliant. Emerson preached the self-improvement and self-importance of the common man. He was deeply concerned with the quality of human life and sincerely believed that the highest quality of life was within the grasp of every man.

A transcendentalist, a romantic poet, a thinker, a seer, a philosopher, a naturalist, a social reformer, a true representative of American Renaissance, Emerson established new traditions in American literature in the nineteenth century. He was more assertive than speculative, more affirmative than sceptical, more suggestive than explanatory. By temperament he was seer like, in expression oracular, in tone scriptural. A pivotal figure in American literary history, Emerson was an ethical thinker as well as an urbane rebel, poet and literary artist.

George Santayana rightly declared that "Emerson's heart was fixed on eternal things and he was in no sense a prophet for his age or country."[74] Matthew Arnold in his book *Discourses in America* attacked the materialism of American Democracy, praised Emerson as "the friend and aider of those who would live in the spirit."[75] He went on to describe Emerson as "the most distinctively and honourably American of our writers."[76] Again his judgment that "we have not in Emerson a great poet, a great writer, but a great philosopher-maker,"[77] has been widely accepted.

Robert Frost maintained that Emerson was one of the greatest Americans. "I suppose" he observed, "I have always thought I would like to name in verse some day my four greatest Americans: George Washington, the General and statesman; Thomas Jefferson, the political thinker, Abraham Lincoln, the martyr and saviour; Ralph Waldo Emerson, the poet."[78] Adapa Ramakrishna Rao said: "Emerson was indeed a *sthita prajna*, a person of steady wisdom or perfect sage, as described in the second chapter of one of his favourite books, the *Bhagvad Gita*."[79]

Emerson was the articulate conscience of the humanity. As we turn over the pages of poetry, essays, and journals, we find ourselves listening to an oracular voice uttering works of gnomic wisdom, in clear but almost expressionless tones.

NOTES

1. This anonymous pamphlet was probably written by Charles Mayo Ellis (1818-1878), "An Essay on Transcendentalism," qtd. W. Harding, "Transcendentalism," *Encyclopedia Americana*, 1965, p. 3.
2. Carl T. Jackson, "Oriental Ideas in American Thought," *Dictionary of the History of Ideas*, ed. Phillip P. Wiener (New York: Charles Scribner's, 1973), III, p. 429.
3. *Works*, Vol. I, p. 29. "Nature."
4. *Ibid.*
5. *The Complete Essays and Other Writings of R.W. Emerson*, p. 87. "The Transcendentalist."
6. *Encyclopedia Americana*, 1965, p. 3.
7. Written after a visit to the Jardinaks Planets in Paris, a famous Botanical and Zoological Garden in 1833.
8. *Works*, Vol. I, p. 5. "Nature."
9. *Ibid.*, p. 10.
10. *Journals*, Vol. IV, p. 34.
11. *Works*, Vol. I, p. 7.
12. *The Letters of Ralph Waldo Emerson*, VI, p. 90.
13. *Ibid.*, VII, p. 218.
14. *Works*, Vol. VII, p. 219. "Books." See also VIII, p. 182.
15. *Journals*, Vol. VIII, p. 34.
16. *Journals*, Vol. VII, p. 511. See also *Works*, Vol. VIII, pp. 215-16.
17. *The Letters of Ralph Waldo Emerson*, I, pp. 116-17.
18. *Works*, Vol. IX, p. 348. "Maia."
19. *Journals*, Vol. IX, p 302.
20. *Ibid.*, Vol. X, p. 159.
21. *Works*, Vol. IX, p. 36. "Hamatreya."
22. *Ibid.*, p. 313. "Illusion."
23. *Journals*, Vol. VII, p. 505.
24. *Ibid.*, p. 159.
25. *Journals*, Vol. VI, p. 189. See also p. 317; VII, p. 8.
26. *Works*, Vol. II, p. 110. "Compensation."
27. *Ibid.*, p. 102.
28. *Ibid.*, Vol. VI, p. 231. "Worship."
29. *Ibid.*
30. *Ibid.*, I, p. 337. "The Transcendentalist."

31. *Works*, Vol. VIII, pp. 342-43. "Immortality."
32. *Journals*, Vol. III, p. 210.
33. *Ibid.*, Vol. VII, p. 94.
34. *Journals*, Vol. VI, p. 494. See also Vol. IX, p. 512.
35. *Works*, Vol. I, pp. 64-65. "Nature."
36. *Emerson Handbook*, p. 118.
37. *Works*, Vol. I, p. 10. "Nature."
38. *Journals*, Vol. III, p. 453.
39. *Works*, Vol. I, p. 216.
40. *Journals*, Vol. III, p. 264.
41. *Ibid.*, Vol. VI, p. 76.
42. *Ibid.*, Vol. VIII, p. 525.
43. *Ibid.*, Vol. V, p. 470.
44. *Works*, Vol. III, p. 171.
45. *Ibid.*, Vol. I, p. 10.
46. *Journals*, Vol. XI, p. 330.
47. *Ibid.*, Vol. II, p. 272.
48. A.G. Macfiffert, ed. *Young Emerson Speaks* (Boston: 1938), p. 209.
49. *Works*, Vol. VIII, p. 65.
50. *Ibid.*, Vol. II, p. 9.
51. *Ibid.*, Vol. I, p. 218.
52. *Ibid.*, Vol. X, p. 134.
53. *Journals*, Vol. II, p. 488.
54. *Ibid.*, Vol. VIII, p. 242.
55. *Ibid.*, Vol. III, p. 235; Vol. V, p. 38; Vol. VI, p. 386; Vol. VIII, p. 456.
56. *Essays*, Vol. II, p. 31.
57. Ronald F. Lee, *Emerson through Kierkegaard*, p. 230.
58. *Works*, Vol. XII, p. 12.
59. *Ibid.*, Vol. I, p. 127.
60. *Ibid.*, p. 122.
61. *Ibid.*, Vol. II, p. 295.
62. *Ibid.*, Vol. I, p. 132.
63. *Ibid.*, p. 127.
64. *Ibid.*, p. 129.
65. *Ibid.*, p. 134.
66. *Works*, Vol. VI, p. 208.
67. *Ibid.*, Vol. V, pp. 258-59; Vol. XII, p. 326.
68. *Ibid.*, Vol. I, p. 83.

69. *Ibid.*, p. 139.
70. *Ibid.*, Vol. X, pp. 226-27. "Preacher."
71. *Ibid.*, Vol. XI, p. 639; Emerson in Concord, p. 170.
72. *Works*, Vol. I, p. 132.
73. *Ibid.*, p. 144.
74. George Santayana, *Interpretations of Poetry and Religion* (New York, 1900), p. 233.
75. Matthew Arnold, *Discourses in America* (New York, 1924), p. 179.
76. *Ibid.*, p. 180.
77. *Ibid.*
78. Robert Frost, *Daedalus* (Fall, 1959), p. 712.
79. Adapa Ramakrishna Rao, *Emerson and Social Reformer* (New Delhi: 1984), p. 110.

Bibliography

Works

The Complete Works of Ralph Waldo Emerson, Centenary ed. 12 Volumes. Boston and New York. 1903-1904.

The Ideal. 4 Vols. New York, 1961.

The Letters of Ralph Waldo Emerson. Ed. Ralph L. Rusk. 6 Vols. New York, 1939.

The Journals and Miscellaneous Notebooks of Ralph Waldo Emerson. Ed. William H. Gilman, Alfred R. Ferguson, George P. Clark, and Merrel R. Davis. (14 Vols. have appeared so far) Cambridge, Mass., 1960.

The Journals of Ralph Waldo Emerson. Ed. Edward W. Emerson and Waldo E. Forbes. 10 Vols. Boston, 1904-14.

The Selected Writings of Ralph Waldo Emerson. Ed. Brooks Atkinson. The Modern Library, New York, 1968.

Uncollected Lectures by Ralph Waldo Emerson. Ed. Clarence Gohdes. New York, 1938.

Uncollected Writings: Essays, Addresses, Poems, Reviews and Letters by Ralph Waldo Emerson. Ed. C.C. Biglow. New York, 1912.

Young Emerson Speaks. Ed. A.C. McGiffert, Jr. Boston, 1938.

Biography

Alcott, Amos B. *Ralph Waldo Emerson: Philosopher and Seer*. Boston, 1882.

Cabot, James Eliot. *A Memoir of Ralph Waldo Emerson*. Boston, 1887.

Cary, Elezabeth Luther. *Emerson, Poet and Thinker*. Concord, Mass. 1903.

Cooke, George Willis. *Ralph Waldo Emerson: His Life, Writings, and Philosophy*. Boston, 1881.

Emerson, Edward Waldo. *Emerson in Concord: A Memoir*. Boston, 1889.

Firkins, Oscar W. *Ralph Waldo Emerson*. Boston, 1915.

Garnett, Richard. *Life of Ralph Waldo Emerson*. London. 1888.

Gray, Robert M. *Emerson: A Study of the Poet as Seer*. New York, 1928.

Guernsey, Alfred H. *Ralph Waldo Emerson: Philosopher and Poet.* New York, 1881.

Holmes, Oliver Wendell. *Ralph Waldo Emerson.* Boston, 1884.

Ireland, Alexander. *Ralph Waldo Emerson: His Life, Genius, and Writings.* London, 1882.

McFiffert, Arthur C. Jr. *Young Emerson Speaks.* Boston, 1938.

Perry, Bliss, *Emerson Today.* Princeton, New Jersey, 1931.

Rusk, Ralph L. *The Life of Ralph Waldo Emerson.* New York, 1929.

Russel, Phillips. *Emerson: The Wisest American.* New York, 1929.

Sanburn, F.B. *The Personality of Emerson.* Boston, 1903.

_____. *The Genius and Character of Emerson,* Boston, 1885.

Searle, Jannuary (George Searle Phillips). *Emerson: His Life and Writings.* London, 1855.

Woodberry, George E. *Ralph Waldo Emerson.* New York, 1907.

Criticism

Benet, W.R. and N.H. Pearson, ed. *The Oxford Anthology of American Literature.* New York, 1963.

Benton, Jeol. *Emerson as a Poet.* New York, 1883.

Bishap, Jonathan. *Emerson on the Soul.* Cambridge Mass., 1964.

Blan, Joseph L. *Men and Movements in American Philosophy.* New York: Prentice Hall, 1953.

Boller, Paul F. *American Transcendentalism, 1830-60: An Intellectual Inquiry.* New York, 1974.

Cameron, K.W. *Emerson among His Contemporaries.* Hartford: Transcendental Books, 1945.

_____. *Young Emerson's Transcendental Vision.* Hartford: Transcendental Books, 1971.

Carpenter, F.I. *Emerson and Asia.* New York, 1953.

Chakravarti, S.C. *The Philosophy of the Upanishads.* Calcutta, 1935.

Chapman, John Jay. *Emerson and Other Essays,* New York, 1898.

Christy, Arthur E., ed. *The Asian Legacy and American Life.* New York, 1968.

_____. *The Orient in American Transcendentalism: A Study of Emerson, Thoreau and Alcott.* New York, Octogood Books, 1963.

Clark, Harry H. *Major American Poets.* New York, 1936.

_____, ed. *Transition in American Literary History.* Curham, N.C., 1953.

Curti, Merie. *The Growth of American Thought.* New Delhi: Tata McGraw Hill, 1964.

Das, S.P. *Emerson's Debt to Hindu Thought: A Reappraisal*. Thesis, Guru Nanak Dev University, Amritsar, 1977.

Detweiler, Robert. *Emerson's Concept of God*. Dissert. University of Florida, 1962.

Dillaway, Newton, *Prophet of American: Emerson and the Problems of Today*. Boston: Little, Brown, 1936.

Duncan, J.L. *The Power and Form of Emerson's Thought*. Charlottesville: Univ. Press of Virginia, 1973.

Foy, R.L.W. *The Philosophy of Ralph Waldo Emerson and its Educational Implications*. Diss. University of Texas, 1962.

Frothingham, O.B., *Transcendentalism in New England: A History*. New York, 1976.

Goddard, H.C. *Studies in New England Transcendentalism*. New York, 1908.

Godman, David, ed. *As You Are: The Teachings of Sri Ramana Maharshi*. Penguin Books, New Delhi. 1985.

Goren, Leyla. *Elements of Brahminism in the Transcendentalism of Emerson*. New York, 1959.

Gould, James Warren. *The First American Contact with Asia*. California: Society for Oriental Studies, 1960.

Gray, H.D. *Emerson: A Statement of New England Transcendentalism as Expressed in the Philosophy of its Chief Exponent*. New York, 1965.

Hiriyana, M. *Outlines of Indian Philosophy*, London: George Allen & Unwin, 1970.

Hume, Robert Ernest. Trans. *The Thirteen Principal Upanishads* (Trans. from the Sanskrit). Oxford University Press, New Delhi, 1983.

Huxley, Aldous. *The Perennial Philosophy*. London: Chatto & Windus, 1947.

Isherwood, Christopher. *An Approach to Vedanta*. Hollywood, Vedanta Press, 1963.

_____, *Vedanta Modern India*. New York: Collier Books, 1962.

_____. Ed. *Vedanta for Western World*. London: George Allen & Unwin, 1949.

James, William. *The Varieties of Religious Experience*. New York: Modern Library, 1902.

Jones, Howard Humford. *Belief and Disbelief in American Literature*. Chicago: University Chicago Press.

Joshi, K.N. *The West Looks at India*. Bareilley: Prakash, 1969.

Karnetts, M.V. *The United States and India, 1776-1976*. Washington, 1976.

Keith, A.B., *The Religion and Philosophy of the Vedas and Upanishads*. Vol. 32. Cambridge, Mass: Harvard University Press, 1925.

Koster, D.N. *Transcendentalism in America*. Boston, 1975.

Krishnamurti, J. *The Awakening of Intelligence*. Avon Books, New York, 1976.

Lal, Chaman. *Hindu America*. Delhi, 1966.

Lavan, Spencer. *Unitarians and India: A Study in Encounter and Response*. Boston: Beacon Press, 1975.

Levin, David, ed. *Emerson: Prophecy, Metamorphosis and Influence*. New York: Columbia University Press, 1975.

Mahadevan, T.M.P. *Ramana Maharshi: The Sage of Arunachala*. A Mandala Book, Unwin Paperbacks, London, 1977.

Matthiesen, F.O. *American Renaissance*. Delhi: Oxford University Press, 1973.

Miller, Perry. *The Transcendentalists*. Cambridge, Mass., 1950.

Narasimhaiah, C.D., ed. *Indian Response to American Literature*. Delhi: Vikas, 1972.

Otto, Rudolf, *Mysticism East and West*. Trans. B.L. Bracey and R.C. Payne. New York: Macmillan, 1972.

Paramananda, Swami. *Emerson and Vedanta*. Boston: Vedanta Centre, 1918.

Patri, Umesh. *Hindu Scriptures and American Transcendentalists*. Intellectual, New Delhi, 1987.

Paul, Sherman. *Emerson's Angle of Vision*. Cambridge, Mass., 1952.

Perry Bliss. *Emerson Today*. Princeton, 1931.

Radhakrishnan, S. *Indian Philosophy*. 2 Vols. London: George Allen & Unwin, 1966.

_____. *The Principal Upanishads*. London: George Allen & Unwin, 1968.

Ramakrishna Rao, Adapa. *Emerson and Social Reform*. New Delhi: Arnold-Heinemann, 1984.

Rayapati, J.P.R. *Early American Interest in Vedanta*. Bombay: Asia, 1973.

Reid, John T. *Indian Influence on American Literature and Thought*. New Delhi: I.C.C.R. 1965.

Scheider, Albert. *The History of American Philosophy*. New York: Columbia University Press, 1947.

Schweitzer, Albert. *Indian Thought and Its Development.* Trans. C.E.D. Russel. London: Adam Charles Black, 1951.

Singh, Man Mohan. *Emerson and India.* Diss. University of Pennsylvania, 1946.

Sircar, Mahendranath. *Hindu Mysticism: According to the Upanishads.* New Delhi: Orient Book Reprint Corporation, 1974.

Stroh, Guy W. *American Philosophy from Edwards to Dewey: An Introduction.* D. Van Nostrand, Princeton, 1968.

Williams, Monier, *Indian Wisdom or Examples of the Religion, Philosophical and Ethical Doctrines of the Hindus.* Delhi: Indian Reprint Public Co., 1974.

Wicke, Mron F. *Emerson's Mysticism.* Western Reserve University, 1946.

Yogananda, Paramahamsa. *Autobiography of a Yogi.* Rider and Company, New York, 1952.

Articles in Foreign Journals

Blan, J.L. "Emerson's Transcendentalist Individualism as a Social Philosophy," *R. Metaphysics*. 31: 80-92, September, 1977.

Brown, S.B. "Emerson's Platonism," *New England Quarterly.* XVIII (1945), 325-45.

Cameroon, K.W. "More Notes on Orientalism in Emerson's Harvard," *ESQ*, 22 (I qrt; 1961).

Carpenter, F.I., "Immortality from India," *American Literature*, I (1929), 233-42.

_____. "William James and Emerson," *American Literature*, XI (March 1939), 39-57.

Cavell, S. "Thinking of Emerson," *New Literary History*, 11, 167-76, Autumn 1979.

Chandran, K.N. "The Pining Gods and Sages in Emerson's Brahma," *English Language Notes*, 27: 55-57, Sept. 1989.

Chandrasekharan, K.R. "Emerson's 'Brahma': And Indian Interpretation," *New England Quarterly*, 23: 4 (December, 1960) 506-12.

Cotkin, G. "R.W. Emerson and William James as Public Philosophers," *Historian*, 49: 49-63, November 1986.

Goodman, R.B. "East-West Philosophy in Nineteenth Century America: Emerson and Hinduism," *Journal of Historical Ideas*, 51: 625-45, October/December, 1990.

Hakergani, Y. "Emerson, Whitman and Zen Buddhism," *Midwest Quarterly*, 31: 433-48, Summer 1990.

Jackson, Carl T. "Oriental Ideas in American Thought," *Dictionary of the History of Ideas*, ed. Phillip P. Wiener. New York, 1973.

Leidecker, K.F. "Emerson and East-West Synthesis," *Philosophy East and West*, I (1951), 40-50.

Leudtke, L.S. "First notices of Emerson in England and Germany, 1935-42," *Notes and Quarterly*, 22: 106-8, March, 1975.

Lindeman, E.C. "Emerson's Pragmatic Mood," *American Scholar*, XVII (1966), 57-64.

Maitra, Herambachandra, "Emerson from an Indian Point of View," *Harvard Theological Review*, 4 (Oct. 1911), 1-15.

Nagarajan, S. "Emerson and Advaita: Some Comparisons and Contrasts," *ATQ*, ns. 3: 325-36, December 1989.

Obuchowski, P.A., "Emerson, Evolution and the Problem of Evil." *Harvard Theological Review*, 1972: 150-56, Jan./April, 1979.

Petry, A.H. "The Meeting of the Twain: Emerson's Hamatreya," *English Language Notes*, 23: 47-52, March 1986.

Pommer, H.F. "The Contents and Basis of Emerson's Belief in Compensation," *PMLA*, LXXVII (1962), 243-53.

Purdy, Vivian. "Emerson's Oriental Philosophy," *Southern University Bulletin*, XLIII (1956), 57-79.

Quinn, P.F. "Emerson and Mysticism," *American Literature*, XXI (1950), 397-414.

Shaw, C.G. "Emerson and Nihilist," *International Journal of Ethics*, XXV (Oct. 1914), 68-86.

Toller, F.B. "Emerson and Quakerism," *American Literature*, X (1938), 142-65.

Wellek, Rene. "Emerson and German Philosophy," *New England Quarterly*, XVI (1943), 41-62.

Whicher, Stephen E. "Emerson's Tragic Senses," *American Scholar*, XXII (1953), 285-92.

White, Robert, L. "Emerson's Brahma," *The Explicator*, XXI (April, 1963), No. 8, Item. 63.

Articles in Indian Journals

Bhattacharjee, M.M. "Ralph Waldo Emerson as a Thinker," *Visvabharati Quarterly*, 21 (Spring, 1956), 400-15.

Das, S.P. "Emerson's Concept of Man," *Literary Criterion*, 8 (2), Summer 1968, 465-70.

_____. "Emerson's Reading in Indian Literature," *Modern Review*, 120 (5), November 1966, 329-34.

Dwivedi, A.N. "Some Vedantic Parallels in Emerson," *Vedic Path*, 44 (4) March, 1982, 36-41.

Dwivedi, R.P. "Emerson's Spiritual Quest and Indian Thought," *Bhavan's Journal*, September 15, 1974, 25-35.

Ezekiel, Nissim, "An Approach to Emerson," *Journal of Literature & Aesthetics*, 2 (1), Jan.-March 1982, 6-12.

Gayatonde, Shakintala N. "Oriental Outlook of Emerson's Philosophy," *Aryan Path*, 38 (3), March 1967, 109-13.

Kanwalli, Sadanad, "Emerson: A Bond between America and India," *The Illustrated Weekly of India*, August 8, 1982, p. 37.

Lal, Inder Jit. "Bewitching Influence of Indian Philosophy on Emerson," *ET*, 25 April 1982, 6:1-6.

_____. "This Famous Writer was Influenced by Indian Philosophy," *The Hindu*, July 23, 1967, Supplement, p. 4.

Nandyal, Ranganath. "India and Emerson," *Triveni*, 55 (2), July-Sept. 1986, 75-77.

Nageswara Rao, E. "Indian Thought in Emerson," *Aryan Path*, 38 (12) December, 1967, 555-57.

Narasimhaiah, C.D., "Transcendentalism in American Literature: An Introductory Essay," *The Literary Criterion*, 5: 3 (Winter 1962) 48-65.

_____. "Nature Makes a Brahmin of Me" *Span*, 23 (December 1982), 12-14.

Patri, Umesh, "Emerson's Brahma in the Light of Gita," *Prabuddha Bharata*, 96 (4), April 1991, 166-69.

Raghavacharyulu, D.V.K. "Indian Influence on American Writers," *Triveni*. 42: 3 (October-December, 1973) 47-53.

Sastri, P.S. "Indian Impact on Emerson," *Indian Scholar*, 1 (2), July, 1979, 93-100.

Seshadri, K. "Echoing Accents: Vedanta and Emerson," *Vedanta Kesari*, 55:1 (May 1968), 42-44.

Sharma, P.P. "Assertion of the Individual; A Recurrent American Theme," *Triveni*, 43: 3 (October-December 1974), 30-36.

Shrivastva, S.N.L. "Emerson's Philosophy of Life," *Aryan Path*, 36 (1), January 1965, 11-16.

Swaminathan, S.R. "The Kathopanishad and Emerson," *Theosophist*, 115 (2) November 1993, 53-57.

Wesley, B.C. "Ralph Waldo Emerson and Indian Thought," *Literary Half-Yearly*, 9 (1), Jan. 1968, 53-65.